THE WEST INDIAN A COMEDY

THE WEST INDIAN

A COMEDY

RICHARD CUMBERLAND

GYAN

Published by

GYAN

Gyan Publishing House
5, Ansari Road
Daryaganj, New Delhi-110002
Phone: 011-47034999, 9811692060
E-mail: books@gyanbooks.com

Distribution Network
gyanbooks.com
India, USA, Canada, UK, Australia

ISBN: 978-93-6780-365-3 (HB)

First Published, 1792

2nd Impression 2024

Printed at: Gyan Press, Delhi.

THE WEST INDIAN A COMEDY
Author: RICHARD CUMBERLAND

THE
WEST INDIAN;
A
COMEDY:

AS IT IS PERFORMED AT THE

THEATRE ROYAL IN DRURY-LANE.

QUIS NOVUS HIC HOSPES?

A NEW EDITION.

LONDON:

PRINTED FOR C. DILLY, IN THE POULTRY.

1792.

DRAMATIS PERSONÆ.

MEN.

Stockwell,	— —	Mr. Aickin.
Belcour,	— —	Mr. King.
Captain Dudley,	—	Mr. Packer.
Charles Dudley,	—	Mr. Cautherly.
Major O'Flaherty,	—	Mr. Moody.
Stukely,	— —	Mr. J. Aickin.
Fulmer,	— —	Mr. Baddely.
Varland,	— —	Mr. Parsons.
Servant to Stockwell,	—	Mr. Wheeler.

WOMEN.

Lady Rusport,	— —	Mrs. Hopkins.
Charlotte Rusport,	—	Mrs. Abington.
Louisa, Daughter to Dudley,		Mrs. Baddely.
Mrs. Fulmer,	— —	Mrs. Egerton.
Lucy,	— —	Mrs. Love.
Housekeeper to Stockwell,	—	Mrs. Bradshaw.

Clerks belonging to Stockwell, servants, sailors, negroes, &c.

SCENE, LONDON.

P R O L O G U E.

SPOKEN BY

MR. R E D D I S H.

CRITICS, hark forward! noble game and new;
A fine Weſt Indian ſtarted full in view:
Hot as the ſoil, the clime, which gave him birth,
You'll run him on a burning ſcent to earth;
Yet don't devour him in his hiding place;
Bag him, he'll ſerve you for another chace;
For ſure that country has no feeble claim,
Which ſwells your commerce, and ſupports your fame.
And in this humble ſketch, we hope you'll find,
Some emanations of a noble mind;
Some little touches, which, tho' void of art,
May find perhaps their way into the heart.
Another hero your excuſe implores,
Sent by your ſiſter kingdom to your ſhores;
Doom'd by Religion's too ſevere command,
To fight for bread againſt his native land:
A brave, unthinking, animated rogue,
With here and there a touch upon the brogue;
Laugh, but deſpiſe him not, for on his lip
His errors lie; his heart can never trip.
Others there are——but may we not prevail
To let the gentry tell their own plain tale?
Shall they come in? They'll pleaſe you, if they can;
If not, condemn the bard—but ſpare the *Man*.
For ſpeak, think, act, or write in angry times,
A wiſh to pleaſe is made the worſt of crimes;
Dire ſlander now with black envenom'd dart,
Stands ever arm'd to ſtab you to the heart.
Rouſe, Britons, rouſe, for honour of your iſle,
Your old good humour; and be ſeen to ſmile.

You

PROLOGUE.

You ſay we write not like our fathers—true,
Nore were our fathers half ſo ſtrict as you,
Damn'd not each error of the poet's pen,
But judging man, remember'd they were men.
Aw'd into ſilence by the times abuſe,
Sleeps many a wiſe, and many a witty muſe;
We that for mere experiment come out,
Are but the light arm'd rangers on the ſcout:
High on Parnaſſus' lofty ſummit ſtands
The immortal camp; there lie the choſen bands!
But give fair quarter to his puny elves,
The giants then will ſally forth themſelves;
With wit's ſharp weapons vindicate the age,
And drive ev'n *Arthur*'s magic from the *Stage*.

THE

WEST INDIAN.

ACT I. SCENE I.

A MERCHANT'S COMPTING HOUSE.

In an inner room, ſet off by glaſs doors, are diſcovered ſeveral clerks, employed at their deſks. A writing table in the front room. STOCKWELL *is diſcovered reading a letter;* STUKELY *comes gently out of the back room, and obſerves him ſome time before he ſpeaks.*

Stukely. HE ſeems diſordered: ſomething in that letter; and I'm afraid of an unpleaſant ſort. He has many ventures of great account at ſea; a ſhip richly freighted for Barcelona; another for Liſbon; and others expected from Cadiz of ſtill greater value. Beſides theſe, I know he has many deep concerns in foreign bottoms, and underwritings to a vaſt amount. I'll accoſt him. Sir! Mr. Stockwell!

Stock. Stukely!—Well, have you ſhip'd the cloths?

Stukely. I have, Sir; here's the bill of lading, and copy of the invoice: the aſſortments are all compared: Mr. Traffick will give you the policy upon 'Change.

Stock. 'Tis very well; lay theſe papers by; and no more of buſineſs for a while. Shut the door, Stukely; I have had long proof of your friendſhip and fidelity to me; a matter of moſt intimate concern lies on my mind, and 'twill be a ſenſible relief to unboſom myſelf to you; I have juſt now been informed of the arrival of the young Weſt Indian, I have ſo long been expecting; you know who I mean.

 Stukely.

Stukely. Yes, Sir; Mr. Belcour, the young gentleman, who inherited old Belcour's great eſtates in Jamaica.

Stock. Huſh, not ſo loud; come a little nearer this way. This Belcour is now in London; part of his baggage is already arrived; and I expect him every minute. Is it to be wonder'd at, if his coming throws me into ſome agitation, when I tell you, Stukely, he is my ſon?

Stukely. Your ſon!

Stock. Yes, Sir, my only ſon; early in life I accompanied his grandfather to Jamaica as his clerk; he had an only daughter, ſomewhat older than myſelf; the mother of this gentleman: it was my chance (call it good or ill) to engage her affections: and, as the inferiority of my condition made it hopeleſs to expect her father's conſent, her fondneſs provided an expedient, and we were privately married; the iſſue of that concealed engagement is, as I have told you, this Belcour.

Stukely. That event, ſurely, diſcovered your connexion.

Stock. You ſhall hear. Not many days after our marriage old Belcour ſet out for England; and, during his abode here, my wife was, with great ſecrecy, delivered of this ſon. Fruitful in expedients to diſguiſe her ſituation, without parting from her infant, ſhe contrived to have it laid and received at her door as a foundling. After ſome time her father returned, having left me here; in one of thoſe favourable moments that decide the fortunes of proſperous men, this child was introduced; from that inſtant, he treated him as his own, gave him his name, and brought him up in his family.

Stukely. And did you never reveal this ſecret, either to old Belcour, or your ſon?

Stock. Never.

Stukely. Therein you ſurprize me; a merchant of your eminence, and a member of the Britiſh parliament, might ſurely aſpire, without offence, to the daughter of a planter. In this caſe too, natural affection would prompt to a diſcovery.

Stock. Your remark is obvious; nor could I have perſiſted in this painful ſilence, but in obedience to the dying injunctions of a beloved wife. This letter, you found me reading, conveyed thoſe injunctions to me; it was dictated in her laſt illneſs, and almoſt in the article of death; (you'll ſpare me the recital of it) ſhe there conjures me, in terms

as

as ſolemn, as they are affecting, never to reveal the ſecret of our marriage, or withdraw my ſon, while her father ſurviv'd.

Stukely. But on what motives did your unhappy lady found theſe injuctions?

Stock. Principally, I believe, from apprehenſion on my account, leſt old Belcour, on whom at her deceaſe I wholly depended, ſhould withdraw his protection: in part from conſideration of his repoſe, as well knowing the diſcovery would deeply affect his ſpirit, which was haughty, vehement, and unforgiving: and laſtly, in regard to the intereſt of her infant, whom he had warmly adopted; and for whom, in caſe of a diſcovery, every thing was to be dreaded from his reſentment. And, indeed, though the alteration in my condition might have juſtified me in diſcovering myſelf, yet I always thought my ſon ſafer in truſting to the caprice than to the juſtice of his grand-father. My judgment has not ſuffered by the event; old Belcour is dead, and has bequeathed his whole eſtate to him we are ſpeaking of.

Stukely. Now then you are no longer bound to ſecrecy.

Stock. True: but before I publicly reveal myſelf, I could wiſh to make ſome experiment of my ſon's diſpoſition: this can only be done by letting his ſpirit take its courſe without reſtraint; by theſe means, I think I ſhall diſcover much more of his real character under the title of his merchant, than I ſhould under that of his father.

SCENE II.

A Sailor enters, uſhering in ſeveral black Servants, carrying portmanteaus, trunks, &c.

Sailor. Save your honour! is your name Stockwell, pray?

Stock. It is.

Sailor. Part of my maſter Belcour's baggage an't pleaſe you; there's another cargo not far a-ſtern of us; and the cockſwain has got charge of the dumb creatures.

Stock. Pr'ythee, friend, what dumb creatures do you ſpeak of; has Mr. Belcour brought over a collection of wild beaſts?

Sailor. No, Lord love him; no, not he: let me ſee; there's two green monkies, a pair of grey parrots, a Jamaica ſow and pigs, and a Mangrove dog; that's all.

Stock. Is that all?

Sailor. Yes, your honour; yes, that's all; bless his heart a'might have brought over the whole island if he would; a didn't leave a dry eye in it.

Stock. Indeed! Stukely, shew 'em where to bestow their baggage. Follow that gentleman.

Sailor. Come, bear a hand, my lads, bear a hand.

[*Exit with* Stukely *and Servants.*

Stock. If the principal tallies with his purveyors, he must be a singular spectacle in this place: he has a friend, however, in this sea-faring fellow; 'tis no bad prognostic of a man's heart, when his ship-mates give him a good word. [*Exit.*

SCENE III.

Scene changes to a drawing-room, a Servant discovered setting the chairs by, &c. a Woman Servant enters to him.

Housek. Why, what a fuss does our good master put himself in about this West Indian: see what a bill of fare I've been forced to draw out: seven and nine I'll assure you, and only a family dinner as he calls it: why if my Lord Mayor was expected, there couldn't be a greater to-do about him.

Servant. I wish to my heart you had but seen the loads of trunks, boxes, and portmanteaus, he has sent hither. An ambassador's baggage, with all the smuggled goods of his family, does not exceed it.

Housek. A fine pickle he'll put the house into: had he been master's own son, and a Christian Englishman, there cou'd not be more rout than there is about this Creolian, as they call 'em.

Servant. No matter for that; he's very rich, and that's sufficient. They say he has rum and sugar enough belonging to him, to make all the water in the Thames into punch. But I see my master's coming. [*Exeunt.*

SCENE IV.

STOCKWELL *enters, followed by a Servant.*

Stock. Where is Mr. Belcour? Who brought this note from him?

Servant.

Servant. A waiter from the London Tavern, Sir; he ſays the young gentleman is juſt dreſt, and will be with you directly.

Stock. Shew him in when he arrives.

Servant. I ſhall, Sir. I'll have a peep at him firſt, however; I've a great mind to ſee this outlandiſh ſpark. The ſailor fellow ſays he'll make rare doings amongſt us. (*aſide*.)

Stock. You need not wait; leave me. [*Exit Servant*. Let me ſee (*reads*.)

"SIR,

"I write to you under the hands of the hair-dreſſer; "as ſoon as I have made myſelf decent, and ſlipped on "ſome freſh cloaths, I will have the honour of paying "you my devoirs.

"Yours,

"BELCOUR."

He write's at his eaſe; for he's unconſcious to whom his letter is addreſſed; but what a palpitation does it throw my heart into; a father's heart! 'Tis an affecting interview; when my eyes meet a ſon, whom yet they never ſaw, where ſhall I find conſtancy to ſupport it? Should he reſemble his mother, I am overthrown. All the letters I have had from him, (for I induſtriouſly drew him into a correſpondence with me) beſpeak him of quick and ready underſtanding. All the reports I ever received, give me favourable impreſſions of his character, wild, perhaps, as the manner of his country is, but, I truſt, not frantic or unprincipled.

SCENE V.

SERVANT *enters*.

Servant. Sir, the foreign gentleman is come.

Another SERVANT.

Servant. Mr. Belcour.

BELCOUR *enters*.

Stock. Mr. Belcour, I'm rejoiced to ſee you; you're welcome to England.

Bel. I thank you heartily, good Mr. Stockwell; you and I have long converſed at a diſtance; now we are met;

met; and the pleaſure this meeting gives me, amply compenſates for the perils I have run through in accompliſhing it.

Stock. What perils, Mr. Belcour? I could not have thought you would have made a bad paſſage at this time o'year.

Bel. Nor did we: courier like, we came poſting to your ſhores, upon the pinions of the ſwifteſt gales that ever blew; 'tis upon Engliſh ground all my difficulties have ariſen; 'tis the paſſage from the river-ſide I complain of.

Stock. Ay, indeed! What obſtructions can you have met between this and the river-ſide?

Bel. Innumerable! Your town's as full of defiles as the Iſland of Corſica; and, I believe, they are as obſtinately defended: ſo much hurry, buſtle, and confuſion, on your quays: ſo many ſugar-caſks, porter-butts, and common council-men, in your ſtreets, that, unleſs a man marched with artillery in his front, 'tis more than the labour of Hercules can effect, to make any tolerable way through your town.

Stock. I am ſorry you have been ſo incommoded.

Bel. Why, faith, 'twas all my own fault: accuſtomed to a land of ſlaves, and out of patience with the whole tribe of cuſtom-houſe extortioners, boat-men, tide-waiters, and water-bailiffs, that beſet me on all ſides, worſe than a ſwarm of muſquetoes, I proceeded a little too roughly to bruſh them away with my rattan; the ſturdy rogues took this in dudgeon, and beginning to rebel, the mob choſe different ſides, and a furious ſcuffle enſued; in the courſe of which, my perſon and apparel ſuffered ſo much, that I was obliged to ſtep into the firſt tavern to refit, before I could make my approaches in any decent trim.

Stock. All without is as I wiſh; dear Nature add the reſt, I am happy *(aſide.)* Well, Mr. Belcour, 'tis a rough ſample you have had of my countrymen's ſpirit; but, I truſt, you'll not think the worſe of them for it.

Bel. Not at all, not at all; I like 'em the better; was I only a viſitor, I might, perhaps, wiſh them a little more tractable; but, as a fellow ſubject, and a ſharer in their freedom, I appland their ſpirit, though I feel the effects of it in every bone of my ſkin.

Stock.

Stock. That's well; I like that well. How gladly I could fall upon his neck, and own myself his father! *(aside.)*

Bel. Well, Mr. Stockwell, for the first time in my life, here am I in England; at the fountain-head of pleasure, in the land of beauty, of arts, and elegancies. My happy stars have given me a good estate, and the conspiring winds have blown me hither to spend it.

Stock. To use it, not to waste it, I should hope; to treat it, Mr. Belcour, not as a vassal, over whom you have a wanton and a despotic power; but as a subject, which you are bound to govern with a temperate and restrained authority.

Bel. True, Sir; most truly said; mine's a commission, not a right: I am the offspring of distress, and every child of sorrow is my brother; while I have hands to hold, therefore, I will hold them open to mankind: but, Sir, my passions are my masters; they take me where they will; and oftentimes they leave to reason and to virtue nothing but my wishes and my sighs.

Stock. Come, come, the man who can accuse corrects himself.

Bel. Ah! that's an office I am weary of: I wish a friend would take it up: I would to Heaven you had leisure for the employ; but, did you drive a trade to the four corners of the world, you would not find the task so toilsome as to keep me free from faults.

Stock. Well, I am not discouraged: this candour tells me I should not have the fault of self-conceit to combat; that, at least, is not amongst the number.

Bel. No; if I knew that man on earth who thought more humbly of me than I do of myself, I would take up his opinion, and forego my own.

Stock. And, was I to choose a pupil, it should be one of your complexion: so if you'll come along with me, we'll agree upon your admission, and enter on a course of lectures directly.

Bel. With all my heart. [*Exeunt.*

SCENE VI.

Scene changes to a room in LADY RUSPORT'*s house.*

LADY RUSPORT *and* CHARLOTTE.

L. Rus. Miss Rusport, I desire to hear no more of Captain Dudley and his destitute family: not a shilling of mine

mine ſhall ever croſs the hands of any of them: becauſe my ſiſter choſe to marry a beggar, am I bound to ſupport him and his poſterity?

Char. I think you are.

L. Ruſ. You think I am; and pray where do you find the law that tells you ſo?

Char. I am not proficient enough to quote chapter and verſe; but I take charity to be a mean clauſe in the great ſtatute of Chriſtianity.

L. Ruſ. I ſay charity, indeed! And pray, Miſs, are you ſure that it is charity, pure charity, which moves you to plead for Captain Dudley? Amongſt all your pity, do you find no ſpice of a certain anti-ſpiritual paſſion, called love? Don't miſtake yourſelf: you are no ſaint, child, believe me; and, I am apt to think, the diſtreſſes of old Dudley, and of his daughter into the bargain, would never break your heart, if there was not a certain young fellow of two and twenty in the caſe; who, by the happy recommendation of a good perſon, and the brilliant appointments of an enſigncy, will, if I am not miſtaken, cozen you out of a fortune of twice twenty thouſand pounds, as ſoon as ever you are of age to beſtow it upon him.

Char. A nephew of your ladyſhip's can never want any other recommendation with me; and, if my partiality for Charles Dudley is acquitted by the reſt of the world, I hope Lady Ruſport will not condemn me for it.

L. Ruſ. I condemn you! I thank Heaven, Miſs Ruſport, I am no ways reſponſible for your conduct; nor is it any concern of mine how you diſpoſe of yourſelf; you are not my daughter; and, when I married your father, poor Sir Stephen Ruſport, I found you a forward ſpoiled Miſs of fourteen, far above being inſtructed by me.

Char. Perhaps your ladyſhip calls this inſtruction.

L. Ruſ. You're ſtrangely pert; but 'tis no wonder: your mother, I'm told was a fine lady; and according to the modern ſtyle of education you was brought up. It was not ſo in my young days; there was then ſome decorum in the world, ſome ſubordination, as the great Locke expreſſes it. Oh! 'twas an edifying ſight, to ſee the regular deportment obſerved in our family: no giggling, no goſſiping was going on there; my good father, Sir Oliver Roundhead, never was ſeen to laugh himſelf, nor ever allowed it in his children.

Char.

Char. Ay; thoſe were happy times, indeed.

L. Ruſ. But, in this forward age, we have coquets in the egg-ſhell, and philoſophers in the cradle; girls of fifteen that lead the faſhion in new caps and new opinions, that have their ſentiments and their ſenſations; and the idle fops encourage 'em in it: O' my conſcience, I wonder what it is the men can ſee in ſuch babies.

Char. True, madam; but all men do not overlook the maturer beauties of your ladyſhip's age, witneſs your admired Major Dennis O'Flaherty; there's an example of ſome diſcernment; I declare to you, when your ladyſhip is by, the Major takes no more notice of me than if I was part of the furniture of your chamber.

L. Ruſ. The Major, child, has travelled through various kingdoms and climates, and has more enlarged notions of female merit than falls to the lot of an Engliſh home-bred lover; in moſt other countries, no woman on your ſide forty would ever be named in a polite circle.

Char. Right, Madam; I've been told that in Vienna they have coquets upon crutches, and Venuſes in their grand climacteric; a lover there celebrates the wrinkles, not the dimples in his miſtreſs's face. The Major, I think, has ſerved in the imperial army.

L. Ruſ. Are you piqu'd, my young madam? Had my ſiſter, Louiſa, yielded to the addreſſes of one of Major O'Flaherty's perſon and appearance, ſhe would have had ſome excuſe: but to run away, as ſhe did, at the age of ſixteen too, with a man of old Dudley's ſort——

Char. Was, in my opinion, the moſt venial treſpaſs that ever girl of ſixteen committed; of a noble family, an engaging perſon, ſtrict honour, and ſound underſtanding, what accompliſhment was there wanting in Captain Dudley, but that which the prodigality of his anceſtors had deprived him of?

L. Ruſ. They left him as much as he deſerves; hasn't the old man captain's half pay? And is not the ſon an enſign?

Char. An enſign! Alas, poor Charles! Would to Heaven he knew what my heart feels and ſuffers for his ſake.

SERVANT *enters.*

Ser. Enſign Dudley to wait upon your ladyſhip.

L. Ruſ. Who! Dudley! What can have brought him to town?

Char. Dear madam, 'tis Charles Dudley, 'tis your nephew.

L. Ruſ. Nephew! I renounce him as my nephew; Sir Oliver renounced him as his grandſon; was'nt he ſon of the eldeſt daughter, and only male deſcendant of Sir Oliver; and didn't he cut him off with a ſhilling? Didn't the poor dear good old man leave his fortune to me, except a ſmall annuity to my maiden ſiſter, who ſpoiled her conſtitution with nurſing him? And, depend upon it, not a penny of that fortune ſhall ever be diſpoſed of otherwiſe than according to the will of the donor. (Charles Dudley *enters.*) So young man, whence came you? What brings you to town?

Charles. If there is any offence in my coming to town, your ladyſhip is in ſome degree reſponſible for it, for part of my errand was to pay my duty here.

L. Ruſ. I hope you have ſome better excuſe than all this.

Charles. 'Tis true, madam, I have other motives; but, if I conſider my trouble repaid by the pleaſure I now enjoy, I ſhould hope my aunt would not think my company the leſs welcome for the value I ſet upon her's.

L. Ruſ. Coxcomb! And where is your father, child; and your ſiſter? Are they in town too?

Charles. They are.

L. Ruſ. Ridiculous! I don't know what people do in London, who have no money to ſpend in it.

Char. Dear madam, ſpeak more kindly to your nephew; how can you oppreſs a youth of his ſenſibility?

L. Ruſ. Miſs Ruſport, I inſiſt upon your retiring to your apartment; when I want your advice I'll ſend to you. (*Exit* Charlotte) So you have put on a red coat too, as well as your father; 'tis plain what value you ſet upon the good advice Sir Oliver uſed to give you; how often has he caution'd you againſt the army?

Charles. Had it pleaſed my grandfather to enable me to have obeyed his caution, I would have done it; but you well know how deſtitute I am; and 'tis not to be wonder'd at if I prefer the ſervice of my king to that of any other maſter.

L. Ruſ. Well, well, take your own courſe; 'tis no concern of mine: you never conſulted me.

Charles.

Charles. I frequently wrote to your ladyſhip, but could obtain no anſwer; and, ſince my grandfather's death, this is the firſt opportunity I have had of waiting upon you.

L. Ruſ. I muſt deſire you not to mention the death of that dear good man in my hearing, my ſpirits cannot ſupport it.

Charles. I ſhall obey you: permit me ſay, that, as that event has richly ſupplied you with the materials of bounty, the diſtreſſes of my family can furniſh you with objects of it.

L. Ruſ. The diſtreſſes of your family, child, are quite out of the queſtion at preſent; had Sir Oliver been pleaſed to conſider them, I ſhould have been well content; but he has abſolutely taken no notice of you in his will, and that to me muſt and ſhall be a law. Tell your father and your ſiſter I totally diſapprove of their coming up to town.

Charles. Muſt I tell my father that before your ladyſhip knows the motive that brought him hither? Allur'd by the offer of exchanging for a commiſſion on full pay, the veteran, after thirty years ſervice, prepares to encounter the fatal heats of Senegambia; but wants a ſmall ſupply to equip him for the expedition.

SERVANT *enters.*

Ser. Major O'Flaherty to wait on your ladyſhip.

MAJOR *enters.*

O'Fla. Spare your ſpeeches, young man; don't you think her ladyſhip can take my word for that? I hope, madam, 'tis evidence enough of my being preſent, when I've the honor of telling you ſo myſelf.

L. Ruſ. Major O'Flaherty, I am rejoiced to ſee you. Nephew Dudley, you perceive I'm engaged.

Charles. I ſhall not intrude upon your ladyſhip's more agreeable engagements. I preſume I have my anſwer.

L. Ruſ. Your anſwer, child! What anſwer can you poſſibly expect; or how can your romantic father ſuppoſe that I am to abet him in all his idle and extravagant undertakings? Come, Major, let me ſhew you the way into my dreſſing-room; and let us leave this young adventurer to his meditation. [*Exit.*

O'Fla. I follow you, my lady. Young gentleman, your obedient! Upon my conſcience, as fine a young fellow as I wou'd wiſh to clap my eyes on: he might have anſwer'd ſwer'd my ſalute, however—well, let it paſs; Fortune, perhaps, frowns upon the poor lad; ſhe's a damn'd ſlippery lady, and very apt to jilt us poor fellows, that wear cockades in our hats. Fare-thee-well, honey, whoever thou art. [*Exit.*

Charles. So much for the virtues of a puritan; out upon it, her heart is flint; yet that woman, that aunt of mine, without one worthy particle in her compoſition, wou'd, I dare be ſworn, as ſoon ſet her foot in a peſt-houſe, as in a play-houſe.

(MISS RUSPORT *enters to him.*)

Char. Stop, ſtay a little, Charles, whither are you going in ſuch haſte?

Charles. Madam; Miſs Ruſport; what are your commands?

Char. Why ſo reſerved? We had uſed to anſwer to no other names than thoſe of Charles and Charlotte.

Charles. What ails you? You've been weeping.

Char. No, no; or if I have—your eyes are full too; but I have a thouſand things to ſay to you: before you go, tell me, I conjure you, where you are to be found; here, give me your direction; write it upon the back of this viſiting-ticket—Have you a pencil?

Charles. I have: but why ſhou'd you deſire to find us out? 'tis a poor little inconvenient place; my ſiſter has no apartment fit to receive you in.

SERVANT *enters.*

Serv. Madam, my lady deſires your company directly.

Char. I am coming—well, have you wrote it? Give it me. O Charles! either you do not, or you will not underſtand me. (*Exeunt ſeverally.*)

END OF THE FIRST ACT.

ACT II. SCENE I.

A Room in Fulmer's House.

Fulmer *and* Mrs. Fulmer.

Mrs. Ful. WHY, how you ſit, muſing and mopeing, ſighing and deſponding! I'm aſhamed of you, Mr. Fulmer: is this the country you deſcribed to me, a ſecond Eldorado, rivers of gold and rocks of diamonds? You found me in a pretty ſnug retir'd way of life at Bologne, out of the noiſe and buſtle of the world, and wholly at my eaſe; you, indeed, was upon the wing, with a fiery perſecution at your back: but like a true ſon of *Loyola*, you had then a thouſand ingenious devices to repair your fortune: and this, your native country was to be the ſcene of your performances: fool that I was, to be inveigled into it by you: but, thank Heaven, our partnerſhip is revocable; I am not your wedded wife, praiſed be my ſtars! for what have we got, whom have we gull'd but ourſelves; which of all your trains has taken fire; even this poor expedient of your bookſeller's ſhop ſeems abandoned; for if a chance cuſtomer drops in, who is there, pray, to help him to what he wants?

Ful. Patty, you know it is not upon ſlight grounds that I deſpair; there had us'd to be a livelihood to be pick'd up in this country, both for the honeſt and diſhoneſt: I have tried each walk, and am likely to ſtarve at laſt: there is not a point to which the wit and faculty of man can turn, that I have not ſet mine to; but in vain, I am beat through every quarter of the compaſs.

Mrs. Ful. Ah! common efforts all: ſtrike me a maſter-ſtroke, Mr. Fulmer, if you wiſh to make any figure in this country.

Ful. But where, how, and what? I have bluſter'd for prerogative; I have bellow'd for freedom; I have offer'd to ſerve my country; I have engaged to betray it; a maſter-ſtroke, truly; why, I have talked treaſon, writ treaſon, and if a man can't live by that he can live by nothing. Here I ſet up as a bookſeller, why men left off reading; and if I was to turn butcher, I believe, o'my conſcience they'd leave off eating.

Capt.

(CAPT. DUDLEY *croſſes the ſtage.*)

Mrs Ful. Why there now's your lodger, old Captain Dudley, as he calls himſelf; there's no flint without fire; ſomething might be ſtruck out of him, if you'd the wit to find the way.

Ful. Hang him, an old dry ſkin'd curmudgeon; you may as well think to get truth out of a courtier, or candour out of a critic: I can make nothing of him; beſides, he's poor, and therefore not for our purpoſe.

Mrs. Ful. The more fool he! Would any man be poor that had ſuch a prodigy in his poſſeſſion?

Ful. His daughter, you mean; ſhe is, indeed, uncommonly beautiful.

Mrs. Ful. Beautiful! Why ſhe need only be ſeen, to have the firſt men in the kingdom at her feet. Egad, I wiſh I had the leaſing of her beauty; what would ſome of our young Nabobs give———?

Ful. Huſh! here comes the Captain; good girl, leave us to ourſelves, and let me try what I can make of him.

Mrs. Ful. Captain, truly! i'faith I'd have a regiment, had I ſuch a daughter, before I was three months older. [*Exit.*

SCENE II.

CAPTAIN DUDLEY *enters to him.*

Ful. Captain Dudley, good morning to you.

Dud. Mr. Fulmer, I have borrowed a book from your ſhop; 'tis the ſixth volume of my deceaſed friend Triſtram; he is a flattering writer to us poor ſoldiers; and the divine ſtory of Le Fevre, which makes part of this book, in my opinion of it, does honour not to its author only, but to human nature.

Ful. He's an author I keep in the way of trade, but one I never reliſh'd: he is much too looſe and profligate for my taſte.

Dud. That's being too ſevere: I hold him to be a moraliſt in the nobleſt ſenſe; he plays indeed with the fancy, and ſometimes perhaps too wantonly; but while he thus deſignedly maſks his main attack, he comes at once upon the heart; refines, amends it, ſoftens it; beats down each ſelfiſh barrier from about it, and opens every ſluice of pity and benevolence.

Ful. We of the catholic perſuaſion are not much bound

to

to him.——Well, Sir, I ſhall not oppoſe your opinion; a favourite author is like a favourite miſtreſs; and there, you know, Captain, no man likes to have his taſte arraigned.

Dud. Upon my word, Sir, I don't know what a man likes in that caſe; 'tis an experiment I never made.

Ful. Sir!—Are you ſerious?

Dud. 'Tis of little conſequence whether you think ſo.

Ful. What a formal old prig it is! (*aſide.*) I apprehend you, Sir; you ſpeak with caution; you are married?

Dud. I have been.

Ful. And this young lady, which accompanies you—

Dud. Paſſes for my daughter.

Ful. Paſſes for his daughter! humph—(*aſide.*) She is exceedingly beautiful, finely accompliſhed, of a moſt enchanting ſhape and air.

Dud. You are much too partial; ſhe has the greateſt defect a woman can have.

Ful. How ſo, pray?

Dud. She has no fortune.

Ful. Rather ſay that you have none; and that's a ſore defect in one of your years, Captain Dudley: you've ſerved, no doubt?

Dud. Familiar coxcomb! But I'll humour him. (*aſide.*)

Ful A cloſe old fox! But I'll unkennel him. (*aſide.*)

Dud. Above thirty years I've been in the ſervice, Mr. Fulmer.

Ful. I gueſs'd as much; I laid it at no leſs: why 'tis a weariſome time; 'tis an apprenticeſhip to a profeſſion, fit only for a patriarch. But preferment muſt be cloſely followed: you never could have been ſo far behind hand in the chace, unleſs you had palpably miſtaken your way. You'll pardon me, but I begin to perceive you have lived in the world, not with it.

Dud. It may be ſo; and you, perhaps, can give me better council. I'm now ſoliciting a favour; an exchange to a company on full pay; nothing more; and yet I meet a thouſand bars to that; tho', without boaſting, I ſhould think the certificate of ſervices, which I ſent in, might have purchaſed that indulgence to me.

Ful. Who thinks or cares about 'em? Certificate of ſervices, indeed! Send in a certificate of your fair daughter; carry her in your hand with you.

Dud.

Dud. What! Who! My daughter! Carry my daughter! Well, and what then?

Ful. Why, then your fortune's made, that's all.

Dud. I underſtand you: and this you call knowledge of the world? Deſpicable knowledge; but, ſirrah, I will have you know—(*threatening him.*)

Ful. Help! Who's within? Wou'd you ſtrike me, Sir? wou'd you lift up your hand againſt a man in his own houſe?

Dud. In a church, if he dare inſult the poverty of a man of honour.

Ful. Have a care what you do; remember there is ſuch a thing in law as an aſſault and battery; ay, and ſuch trifling forms as warrants and indictments.

Dud. Go, Sir; you are too mean for my reſentment: 'tis that, and not the law, protects you. Hence!

Ful. An old, abſurd, incorrigible blockhead! I'll be reveng'd of him. (*aſide.*)

SCENE III.

YOUNG DUDLEY *enters* to *him.*

Charles. What is the matter, Sir? Sure I heard an outcry as I enter'd the houſe.

Dud. Not unlikely; our landlord and his wife are for ever wrangling.—Did you find your aunt Dudley at home?

Charles. I did.

Dud. And what was your reception?

Charles. Cold as our poverty and her pride could make it.

Dud. You told her the preſſing occaſion I had for a ſmall ſupply to equip me for this exchange; has ſhe granted me the relief I aſked?

Charles. Alas! Sir, ſhe has peremptorily refuſed it.

Dud. That's hard; that's hard, indeed! My petition was for a ſmall ſum; ſhe has refuſed it, you ſay: well, be it ſo; I muſt not complain. Did you ſee the broker about the inſurance on my life?

Charles. There again I am the meſſenger of ill news; I can raiſe no money, ſo fatal is the climate: alas! that ever my father ſhould be ſent to periſh in ſuch a place!

SCENE IV.

MISS DUDLEY *enters haſtily.*

Dud. Louiſa, what's the matter? you ſeem frighted.

Lou.

Lou. I am, indeed: coming from Miſs Ruſport's, I met a young gentleman in the ſtreets, who has beſet me in the ſtrangeſt manner.

Charles. Inſufferable! Was he rude to you?

Lou. I cannot ſay he was abſolutely rude to me, but he was very importunate to ſpeak to me, and once or twice attempted to lift up my hat; he follow'd me to the corner of the ſtreet, and there I gave him the ſlip.

Dud. You muſt walk no more in the ſtreets, child, without me, or your brother.

Lou. O Charles! Miſs Ruſport deſires to ſee you directly; Lady Ruſport is gone out, and ſhe has ſomething particular to ſay to you.

Charles. Have you any commands for me, Sir?

Dud. None, my dear; by all means wait upon Miſs Ruſport. Come, Louiſa; I ſhall deſire you to go up to your chamber, and compoſe yourſelf. [*Exeunt.*

SCENE V.

BELCOUR *enters, after peeping in at the door.*

Bel. Not a ſoul, as I'm alive. Why, what an odd ſort of a houſe is this! Confound the little jilt, ſhe has fairly given me the ſlip. A plague upon this London, I ſhall have no luck in it: ſuch a crowd and ſuch a hurry, and ſuch a number of ſhops, and one ſo like the other, that whether the wench turn'd into this houſe or the next, or whether ſhe went up ſtairs or down ſtairs, (for there's a world above and a world below, it ſeems) I declare, I know no more than if I was in the Blue Mountains. In the name of all the devils at once, why did ſhe run away? If every handſome girl I meet in this town is to lead me ſuch a wild-gooſe chace, I had better have ſtay'd in the torrid zone: I ſhall be waſted to the ſize of a ſugar-cane: what ſhall I do? give the chace up? hang it, that's cowardly: ſhall I, a true-born ſon of Phœbus, ſuffer this little nimble-footed Daphne to eſcape me?——"Forbid it honour, and forbid it love." Huſh! huſh! here ſhe comes! Oh! the devil! What tawdry thing have we got here?

MRS. FULMER *enters to him.*

Mrs. Ful. Your humble ſervant, Sir.

Bel. Your humble ſervant, Madam.

Mrs. Ful. A fine ſummer's day, Sir.

Bel. Yes, Ma'am, and ſo cool, that if the calendar didn't call it July, I ſhould ſwear it was January.

Mrs. Ful. Sir!.

Bel. Madam!

Mrs. Ful. Do you wiſh to ſpeak to Mr. Fulmer, Sir?

Bel. Mr. Fulmer, Madam? I havn't the honour of knowing ſuch a perſon.

Mrs. Ful. No, I'll be ſworn, have you not; thou art much too pretty a fellow, and too much of a gentleman, to be an author thyſelf, or to have any thing to ſay to thoſe that are ſo. 'Tis the Captain, I ſuppoſe, you are waiting for.

Bel. I rather ſuſpect it is the Captain's wife.

Mrs. Ful. The Captain has no wife, Sir.

Bel. No wife! I'm heartily ſorry for it; for then ſhe's his miſtreſs; and that I take to be the more deſperate caſe of the two: pray, Madam, wasn't there a lady juſt now turn'd into your houſe? 'Twas with her I wiſhed to ſpeak.

Mrs. Ful. What ſort of a lady, pray?

Bel. One of the lovelieſt ſort my eyes ever beheld; young, tall, freſh, fair; in ſhort, a goddeſs.

Mrs Ful. Nay, but dear, dear Sir, now I'm ſure you flatter; for 'twas me you followed into the ſhop door this minute.

Bel. You! No, no, take my word for it, it was not you, Madam.

Mrs. Ful. But what is it you laugh at?

Bel. Upon my ſoul, I aſk your pardon; but it was not you, believe me; be aſſur'd it wasn't.

Mrs. Ful. Well, Sir, I ſhall not contend for the honour of being notic'd by you; I hope you think you woudn't have been the firſt man that notic'd me in the ſtreets; however, this I'm poſitive of, that no living woman but myſelf has enter'd theſe doors this morning.

Bel. Why then I'm miſtaken in the houſe, that's all; for 'tis not humanly poſſible I can be ſo far out in the lady, *(going)*

Mrs. Ful. Coxcomb! But hold—a thought occurs; as ſure as can be he has ſeen Miſs Dudley. A word with you, young gentleman; come back.

Bel. Well, what's your pleaſure?

Mrs. Ful. You ſeem greatly captivated with this young lady; are you apt to fall in love thus at firſt ſight?

Bel. Oh, yes: 'tis the only way I can ever fall in love any man may tumble into a pit by ſurpriſe, none but a fool would walk into one by choice.

Mrs. Ful. You are a haſty lover it ſeems; have you ſpirit to be a generous one? They that will pleaſe the eye muſtn't ſpare the purſe.

Bel. Try me; put me to the proof; bring me to an interview with the dear girl that has thus captivated me, and ſee whether I have ſpirit to be grateful.

Mrs. Ful. But how, pray, am I to know the girl you have ſet your heart on?

Bel. By an undeſcribable grace, that accompanies every look and action that falls from her; there can be but one ſuch woman in the world, and nobody can miſtake that one.

Mrs. Ful. Well, if I ſhould ſtumble upon this angel in my walks, where am I to find you? What's your name?

Bel. Upon my ſoul I can't tell you my name.

Mrs. Ful. Not tell me! Why ſo?

Bel. Becauſe I don't know what it is myſelf; as yet I have no name.

Mrs. Ful. No name!

Bel. None; a friend, indeed, lent me his; but he forbad me to uſe it on any unworthy occaſion.

Mrs. Ful. But where is your place of abode?

Bel. I have none; I never ſlept a night in England in my life.

Mrs. Ful. Hey-day!

SCENE VI.

FULMER *enters.*

Ful. A fine caſe, truly, in a free country; a pretty paſs things are come to, if a man is to be aſſaulted in his own houſe.

Mrs. Ful. Who has aſſaulted you, my dear?

Ful. Who! why this Captain Drawcanſir, this old Dudley, my lodger; but I'll unlodge him; I'll unharbour him, I warrant.

Mrs. Ful. Huſh! huſh! Hold your tongue man; pocket the affront, and be quiet; I've a ſcheme on foot will pay you a hundred beatings. Why you ſurprize me, Mr. Fulmer; Captain Dudley aſſault you! Impoſſible.

Ful. Nay, I can't call it an abſolute aſſault; but he threatened me.

Mrs. Ful. Oh, was that all? I thought how it would turn out—A likely thing, truly, for a perſon of his obliging compaſſionate turn: no, no, poor Captain Dudley, he has ſorrows and diſtreſſes enough of his own to employ his ſpirits, without ſetting them againſt other people. Make it up as faſt as you can: watch this gentleman out; follow him wherever he goes; and bring me word who and what he is; be ſure you don't loſe ſight of him; I've other buſineſs in hand. *Exit.*]

Bel. Pray, Sir, what ſorrows and diſtreſſes have befallen this old Gentleman you ſpeak of?

Ful. Poverty, diſappointment, and all the diſtreſſes attendant thereupon: ſorrow enough of all conſcience: I ſoon found how it was with him by his way of living, low enough of all reaſon; but what I overheard this morning put it out of all doubt.

Bel. What did you overhear this morning?

Ful. Why, it ſeems he wants to join his regiment, and has been beating the town over to raiſe a little money for that purpoſe upon his pay; but the climate, I find, where he is going, is ſo unhealthy, that nobody can be found to lend him any.

Bel. Why then your town is a damn'd good for-nothing town: and I wiſh I had never come into it.

Ful. That's what I ſay, Sir; the hard-heartedneſs of ſome folks is unaccountable. There's an old Lady Ruſport, a near relation of this gentleman's; ſhe lives hard by here, oppoſite to Stockwell's, the great merchant; he ſent to her a begging, but to no purpoſe; though ſhe is as rich as a Jew, ſhe would not furniſh him with a farthing.

Bel. Is the Captain at home?

Ful. He is up ſtairs, Sir,

Bel. Will you take the trouble to deſire him to ſtep hither? I want to ſpeak to him.

Ful. I'll ſend him to you directly. I don't know what to make of this young man; but, if I live, I will find him out, or know the reaſon why. [*Exit.*

Bel. I've loſt the girl it ſeems; that's clear: ſhe was the firſt object of my purſuit; but the caſe of this poor officer touches me; and, after all, there may be as much true delight in reſcuing a fellow creature from diſtreſs, as there would

would be in plunging one into it——But let me ſee; it's a point that muſt be managed with ſome delicacy—A propos! there's pen and ink—I've ſtruck upon a method that will do (*writes.*) Ay, ay, this is the very thing: 'twas deviliſh lucky I happen'd to have theſe bills about me. There, there, fare you well; I'm glad to be rid of you; you ſtood a chance of being worſe applied, I can tell you (*encloſes and ſeals the paper.*)

SCENE VII.

FULMER *brings in* DUDLEY.

Ful. That's the gentleman, Sir. I ſhall make bold, however, to lend an ear.

Dud. Have you any commands for me, Sir?

Bel. Your name is Dudley, Sir——?

Dud. It is.

Bel. You command a company, I think, Captain Dudley?

Dud. I did: I am now upon half-pay.

Bel. You've ſerv'd ſome time?

Dud. A pretty many years; long enough to ſee ſome people of more merit, and better intereſt than myſelf, made general officers.

Bel. Their merit I may have ſome doubt of; their intereſt I can readily give credit to; there is little promotion to be looked for, in your profeſſion, I believe, without friends, Captain?

Dud. I believe ſo too: have you any other buſineſs with me, may I aſk?

Bel. Your patience for a moment. I was informed you was about to join your regiment in diſtant quarters abroad.

Dud. I have been ſoliciting an exchange to a company on full-pay, quarter'd at James's-Fort, in Senegambia; but, I'm afraid, I muſt drop the undertaking.

Bel. Why ſo, pray?

Dud. Why ſo, Sir? 'Tis a home-queſtion for a perfect ſtranger to put; there is ſomething very particular in all this.

Bel. If it is not impertinent, Sir, allow me to aſk you what reaſon you have for deſpairing of ſucceſs.

Dud. Why really, Sir, mine is an obvious reaſon for a ſoldier to have—Want of money; ſimply that.

Bel.

Bel. May I beg to know the ſum you have occaſion for?

Dud. Truly, Sir, I cannot exactly tell you on a ſudden; nor is it, I ſuppoſe, of any great conſequence to you to be informed; but I ſhould gueſs, in the groſs, that two hundred pounds would ſerve.

Bel. And do you find a difficulty in raiſing that ſum upon your pay? 'Tis done every day.

Dud. The nature of the climate makes it difficult: I can get no one to inſure my life.

Bel. Oh! that's a circumſtance may make for you, as well as againſt: in ſhort Captain Dudley, it ſo happens, that I can command the ſum of two hundred pounds: ſeek no farther; I'll accomodate you with it upon eaſy terms.

Dud. Sir! do I underſtand you rightly?—I beg your pardon; but am I to believe that you are in earneſt?

Bel. What is your ſurprize? Is it an uncommon thing for a gentleman to ſpeak truth? Or is it incredible that one fellow creature ſhould aſſiſt another?

Dud. I aſk your pardon—May I beg to know to whom? Do you propoſe this in the way of buſineſs?

Bel. Entirely: I have no other buſineſs on earth.

Dud. Indeed! you are not a broker, I'm perſuaded.

Bel. I am not.

Dud. Nor an army agent I think?

Bel. I hope you will not think the worſe of me for being neither; in ſhort, Sir, if you will peruſe this paper, it will explain to you who I am, and upon what terms I act; while you read it, I will ſtep home, and fetch the money: and we will conclude the bargain without loſs of time. In the mean while, good day to you. [*Exit haſtily.*

Dud. Humph! there's ſomething very odd in all this—let me ſee what we've got here—This paper is to tell me who he is, and what are his terms: in the name of wonder, why has he ſealed it! Hey dey! what's here? Two Bank notes, of a hundred each! I can't comprehend what this means. Hold; here's a writing; perhaps that will ſhow me. " Accept this trifle; purſue your fortune, and proſper." Am I in a dream? Is this a reality?

SCENE VIII.

Enter MAJOR O'FLAHERTY.

Ma. Save you, my dear! Is it you now that are Captain Dudley, I would aſk?——Whuh! What's the hurry the

man's

man's in? If 'tis the lad that run out of the shop you would overtake, you might as well stay where you are; by my soul he's as nimble as a Croat, you are a full hour's march in his rear—Ay, faith, you may as well turn back, and give over the pursuit; well, Captain Dudley, if that's your name, there's a letter for you. Read, man; read it; and I'll have a word with you after you have done.

Dud. More miracles on foot! So, so, from Lady Rusport.

O'Fla. You're right; it's from her ladyship.

Dud. Well, Sir, I have cast my eye over it; 'tis short and peremptory; are you acquainted with the contents?

O'Fla. Not at all, my dear; not at all.

Dud. Have you any message from Lady Rusport?

O'Fla. Not a syllable, honey: only, when you've digested the letter, I've a little bit of a message to deliver you from myself.

Dud. And may I beg to know who yourself is?

O'Fla. Dennis O'Flaherty, at your service; a poor major of grenadiers; nothing better.

Dud. So much for your name and title, Sir; now be so good to favour me with your message.

O'Fla. Why then, Captain, I must tell you I have promised Lady Rusport you shall do whatever it is she bids you to do in that letter there.

Dud. Ay, indeed; have you undertaken so much, Major, without knowing either what she commands, or what I can perform?

O'Fla. That's your concern, my dear, not mine; I must keep my word, you know.

Dud. Or else, I suppose, you and I must measure swords.

O'Fla. Upon my soul you've hit it.

Dud. That would hardly answer to either of us; you and I have, probably, had enough of fighting in our time before now.

O'Fla. Faith and troth, Master Dudley, you may say that; 'tis thirty years, come the time, that I have followed the trade, and in a pretty many countries.—Let me see—In the war before last I serv'd in the Irish brigade, d'ye see; there, after bringing off the French monarch, I left his service, with a British bullet in my body, and this ribband in my button-hole. Last war I followed the fortunes of the German eagle, in the corps of grenadiers; there I had my belly full of fighting, and a plentiful scarcity of every thing

thing elſe. After ſix and twenty engagements, great and ſmall, I went off with this gaſh on my ſcull, and a kiſs of the Empreſs Queen's ſweet hand, (Heaven bleſs it!) for my pains. Since, the peace, my dear, I took a little turn with the Confederates there in Poland—but ſuch another ſet of madcaps!—by the lord Harry, I never knew what it was they were ſcuffling about.

Dud. Well, Major, I won't add another action to the liſt, you ſhall keep your promiſe with Lady Ruſport; ſhe requires me to leave London; I ſhall go in a few days, and you may take what credit you pleaſe from my compliance.

O'Fla. Give me your hand, my dear boy! this will make her my own; when that's the caſe, we ſhall be brothers, you know, and we'll ſhare her fortune between us.

Dud. Not ſo, Major; the man who marries Lady Ruſport will have a fair title to her whole fortune without diviſion. But, I hope, your expectations of prevailing are founded upon good reaſons.

O'Fla. Upon the beſt grounds in the world; firſt, I think ſhe will comply, becauſe ſhe is a woman; ſecondly, I am perſuaded ſhe won't hold out long, becauſe ſhe's a widow: and thirdly, I make ſure of her, becauſe I've married five wives, (*en militaire,* Captain) and never failed yet; and, for what I know, they're all alive and merry at this very hour.

Dud. Well, Sir, go on and proſper, if you can inſpire Lady Ruſport with half your charity, I ſhall think you deſerve all her fortune; at preſent, I muſt beg your excuſe: good morning to you. [*Exit.*

O'Fla. A good ſenſible man, and very much of a ſoldier; I did not care if I was better acquainted with him: but 'tis an aukward kind of country for that; the Engliſh, I obſerve, are cloſe friends, but diſtant acquaintance. I ſuſpect the old lady has not been over-generous to poor Dudley; I ſhall give her a little touch about that: upon my ſoul, I know but one excuſe a perſon can have for giving nothing, and that is, like myſelf, having nothing to give. [*Exit.*

SCENE IX.

Scene changes to LADY RUSPORT'S *houſe. A dreſſing-room.*

MISS RUSPORT *and* LUCY.

Char. Well, Lucy, you've diſlodg'd the old lady at laſt; but methought you was a tedious time about it.

Lucy.

Lucy. A tedious time, indeed; I think they who have least to spare, contrive to throw the most away, I thought I shou'd never have got her out of the house.

Char. Why, she's as deliberate in canvassing every article of her dress, as an ambassador would be in settling the preliminaries of a treaty.

Lucy. There was a new hood and handkerchief, that had come express from Holborn-Hill on the occasion, that took as much time in adjusting——

Char. As they did in making, and she was as vain of them as an old maid of a young lover.

Lucy. Or a young lover of himself. Then, madam, this being a visit of great ceremony to a person of distinction, at the West end of the town, the old state chariot was dragg'd forth on the occasion, with strict charges to dress out the box with the leopard-skin hammer-cloth.

Char. Yes, and to hang the false tails on the miserable stumps of the old crawling cattle. Well, well, pray Heaven the crazy affair don't break down again with her! at least till she gets to her journey's end.——But where's Charles Dudley? Run down, dear girl, and be ready to let him in; I think he's as long in coming as she was in going.

Lucy. Why, indeed, Madam, you seem the more alert of the two, I must say. [*Exit*.

Char. Now the deuce take the girl for putting that notion into my head: I'm sadly afraid Dudley does not like me; so much encouragement as I have given him to declare himself, I never could get a word from him on the subject! This may be very honourable, but upon my life it's very provoking. By the way, I wonder how I look to day: Oh! shockingly! hideously pale! like a witch! This is the old lady's glass; and she has left some of her wrinkles on it. How frightfully have I put on my cap! all awry! and my hair dress'd so unbecoming! altogether, I'm a most complete fright.

SCENE X.

(CHARLES DUDLEY *comes in unobserved*.)

Charles. That I deny.

Char. Ah!

Charles. Quarrelling with your glass, cousin? Make it

up; make it up and be friends; it cannot compliment you more than by reflecting you as you are.

Char. Well, I vow, my dear Charles, that is delightfully faid, and deferves my very beft curt'fy: your flattery, like a rich jewel, has a value not only from its fuperior luftre, but from its extraordinary fcarcenefs: I verily think this is the only civil fpeech you ever directed to my perfon in your life.

Charles. And I ought to afk pardon of your good fenfe for having done it now.

Char. Nay, now you relapfe again: don't you know, if you keep well with a woman on the great fcore of beauty, fhe'll never quarrel with you on the trifling article of good fenfe? But any thing ferves to fill up a dull yawning hour with an infipid coufin; you have brighter moments, and warmer fpirits, for the dear girl of your heart.

Charles. Oh! fie upon you, fie upon you.

Char. You blufh, and the reafon is apparent: you are a novice at hypocrify; but no practice can make a vifit of ceremony pafs for a vifit of choice: love is ever before its time; friendfhip is apt to lag a little after it; pray, Charles, did you make any extraordinary hafte hither?

Charles. By your queftion, I fee you acquit me of the impertinence of being in love.

Char. But why impertinence? Why the impertinence of being in love? You have one language for me, Charles, and another for the woman of your affection.

Charles. You are miftaken; the woman of my affection fhall never hear any other language from me than what I ufe to you.

Char. I am afraid then you'll never make yourfelf underftood by her.

Charles. It is not fit I fhould; there is no need of love to make me miferable; 'tis wretchednefs enough to be a beggar.

Char. A beggar, do you call yourfelf! O Charles, Charles, rich in every merit and accomplifhment, whom may you not afpire to? And why think you fo unworthily of our fex, as to conclude there is not one to be found with fenfe to difcern your virtue, and generofity to reward it?

Charles. You diftrefs me; I muft beg to hear no more.

Char. Well, I can be filent.——Thus does he always ferve me, whenever I am about to difclofe myfelf to him.

Charles.

Charles. Why do you not banifh me and my misfortunes for ever from your thoughts?

Char. Ay, wherefore do I not, fince you never allowed me a place in yours? But go, Sir, I have no right to ftay you; go where your heart directs you; go to the happy, the diftinguifhed fair one.

Charles. Now, by all that's good, you do me wrong; there is no fuch fair one for me to go to, nor have I an acquaintance among the fex, yourfelf excepted which anfwers to that defcription.

Char. Indeed!

Charles. In very truth: there then let us drop the fubject. May you be happy, though I never can!

Char. O Charles! give me your hand, if I have offended you, I afk your pardon: you have been long acquainted with my temper, and know how to bear with its infirmities.

Char. Thus, my dear Charlotte, let us feal our reconciliation (*kiffing her hand*) Bear with thy infirmities! By Heaven, I know not any one failing in thy whole compofition, except that of too great a partiality for an undeferving man.

Char. And you are now taking the very courfe to augment that failing. A thought ftrikes me: I have a commiffion that you muft abfolutely execute for me; I have immediate occafion for the fum of two hundred pounds; you know my fortune is fhut up till I am of age; take this paltry box, (it contains my ear-rings, and fome other baubles I have no ufe for) carry it to our oppofite neighbour, Mr. Stockwell, (I don't know where elfe to apply) leave it as a depofit in his hands, and beg him to accommodate me with the fum.

Charles. Dear Charlotte, what are you about to do? How can you poffibly want two hundred pounds?

Char. How can I poffibly do without it, you mean? Doesn't every lady want two hundred pounds? Perhaps I have loft it at play; perhaps I mean to win as much to it; perhaps I want it for two hundred different ufes.

Charles. Pooh! pooh! all this is nothing; don't I know you never play?

Char. You miftake; I have a fpirit to fet not only this trifle, but my whole fortune, upon a ftake; therefore make no wry faces, but do as I bid you: you will find Mr. Stockwell a very honourable gentleman.

LUCY *enters in haste.*

Lucy. Dear madam, as I live, here comes the old lady in a hackney-coach.

Char. The old chariot has given her a second tumble; away with you; you know your way out without meeting her: take the box, and do as I desire you.

Charles. I must not dispute your orders. Farewell!

[*Exeunt* CHARLES *and* CHARLOTTE.

SCENE XI.

LADY RUSPORT *enters, leaning on* MAJOR O'FLAHERTY'S *arm.*

O'Fla. Rest yourself upon my arm; never spare it; 'tis strong enough; it has stood harder service than you can put it too.

Lucy. Mercy upon me, what is the matter: I am frighten'd out of my wits: has your ladyship had an accident?

L. Rus. O Lucy; the most untoward one in nature: I know not how I shall repair it.

O'Fla. Never go about to repair it, my lady; ev'n build a new one; 'twas but a crazy piece of business at best.

Lucy. Bless me, is the old chariot broke down with you again?

L Rus. Broke, child? I don't know what might have been broke, if, by great good fortune, this obliging gentleman had not been at hand to assist me.

Lucy. Dear madam, let me run and fetch you a cup of the cordial drops.

L. Rus. Do, Lucy. Alas! Sir, ever since I lost my husband, my poor nerves have been shook to pieces: there hangs his beloved picture; that precious relick, and a plentiful jointure, is all that remains to console me for the best of men.

O'Fla. Let me see; i'faith a comely personage; by his fur cloak I suppose he was in the Russian service; and by the gold chain round his neck, I should guess he had been honoured with the order of St. Catharine.

L. Rus. No, no; he meddled with no St. Catharines: that's the habit he wore in his mayoralty; Sir Stephen was Lord-Mayor of London: but he is gone, and has left me a poor, weak, solitary widow behind him.

O'Fla.

O'Fla. By all means, then, take a ſtrong, able, hearty man to repair his loſs: if ſuch a plain fellow as one Dennis O'Flaherty can pleaſe you, I think I may venture to ſay, without any diſparagement to the gentleman in the fur gown there——

L. Ruſ. What are you going to ſay? Don't ſhock my ears with any compariſons, I deſire.

O'Fla. Not I, by my ſoul; I don't believe there's any compariſon in the caſe.

L. Ruſ Oh, are you come? Give me the drops; I'm all in a flutter.

O'Fla. Hark'e, ſweetheart, what are thoſe ſame drops? Have you any more left in the bottle? I didn't care if I took a little ſip of them myſelf.

Lucy. Oh, Sir, they are called the cordial reſtorative elixir, or the nervous golden drops; they are only for ladies caſes.

O'Fla. Yes, yes, my dear, there are gentlemen as well as ladies that ſtand in need of thoſe ſame golden drops; they'd ſuit my caſe to a tittle.

L. Ruſ. Well, Major, did you give old Dudley my letter, and will the ſilly man do as I bid him, and be gone?

O'Fla. You are obey'd; he's on his march.

L. Ruſ. That's well; you have manag'd this matter to perfection; I didn't think he would have been ſo eaſily prevail'd upon.

O'Fla. At the firſt word; no difficulty in life; 'twas the very thing he was determined to do, before I came; I never met a more obliging gentleman.

L. Ruſ. Well, 'tis no matter; ſo I am but rid of him, and his diſtreſſes: wou'd you believe it, Major O'Flaherty, it was but this morning he ſent a begging to me for money to fit him out upon ſome wild-gooſe expedition to the coaſt of Africa, I know not where.

O'Fla. Well, you ſent him what he wanted?

L. Ruſ. I ſent him what he deſerv'd, a flat refuſal.

O'Fla. You refuſed him?

L. Ruſ. Moſt undoubtedly.

O'Fla. You ſent him nothing!

L. Ruſ. Not a ſhilling.

O'Fla. Good morning to you—Your ſervant—(*going.*)

L. Ruſ. Hey-day! What ails the man? Where are you going?

O'Fla.

O'Fla. Out of your houſe, before the roof falls on my head—to poor Dudley, to ſhare the little modicum that thirty years hard ſervice has left me; I wiſh it was more for his ſake.

L. Ruſ. Very well, Sir; take your courſe; I ſhan't attempt to ſtop you; I ſhall ſurvive it; it will not break my heart if I never ſee you more.

O'Fla. Break your heart! No, o'my conſcience will it not.—You preach, and you pray, and you turn up your eyes, and all the while you're as hard-hearted as an hyena—A hyena, truly! By my ſoul there isn't in the whole creation ſo ſavage an animal as a human creature without pity. [*Exit.*

L. Ruſ. A hyena, truly! Where did the fellow blunder upon that word? Now the deuce take him for uſing it, and the Macaronies for inventing it.

END OF THE SECOND ACT.

ACT

ACT III. SCENE I.

A Room in STOCKWELL's *House.*

STOCKWELL *and* BELCOUR.

Stock. GRATIFY me ſo far, however, Mr. Belcour, as to ſee Miſs Ruſport; carry her the ſum ſhe wants, and return the poor girl her box of diamonds, which Dudley left in my hands; you know what to ſay on the occaſion better than I do; that part of your commiſſion I leave to your own diſcretion, and you may ſeaſon it with what gallantry you think fit.

Bel. You cou'd not have pitch'd upon a greater bungler at gallantry than myſelf, if you had rummag'd every company in the city, and the whole court of aldermen into the bargain: part of your errand, however, I will do; but whether it ſhall be with an ill grace or a good one, depends upon the caprice of a moment, the humour of the lady, the mode of our meeting, and a thouſand undefinable ſmall circumſtances that nevertheleſs determine us upon all the great occaſions of life.

Stock. I perſuade myſelf you will find Miſs Ruſport an ingenious, worthy, animated girl.

Bel. Why I like her the better, as a woman; but name her not to me as a wife! No, if ever I marry, it muſt be a ſtaid, ſober, conſiderate damſel, with blood in her veins as cold as a turtle's; quick of ſcent as a vulture when danger's in the wind; wary and ſharp-ſighted as a hawk when treachery is on foot: with ſuch a companion at my elbow, for ever whiſpering in my ear—have a care of this man, he's a cheat; don't go near that woman, ſhe's a jilt; over head there's a ſcaffold, under foot there's a well: Oh! Sir, ſuch a woman might lead me up and down this great city without difficulty or danger; but with a girl of Miſs Ruſport's complexion, heaven and earth, Sir! we ſhould be dup'd, undone, and diſtracted, in a fortnight.

Stock Ha! ha! ha! Why you are become wond'rous circumſpect of a ſudden, pupil; and if you can find ſuch a prudent damſel as you deſcribe, you have my conſent—only beware how you chooſe; diſcretion is not the reigning quality amongſt the fine ladies of the preſent time; and I think

I think in Miſs Ruſport's particular I have given you no bad counſel.

Bel. Well, well, if you'll fetch me the jewels, I believe I can undertake to carry them to her; but as for the money, I'll have nothing to do with that; Dudley would be your fitteſt ambaſſador on that occaſion; and, if I miſtake not, the moſt agreeable to the lady.

Stock. Why, indeed, from what I know of the matter, it may not improbably be deſtined to find its way into his pockets. [*Exit.*

Bel. Then, depend upon it, theſe are not the only trinkets ſhe means to dedicate to Captain Dudley. As for me, Stockwell indeed wants me to marry; but till I can get this bewitching girl, this incognita, out of my head, I can never think of any other woman.

(SERVANT *enters, and delivers a letter.*)

Heyday! Where can I have picked up a correſpondent already! 'Tis a moſt execrable manuſcript—Let me ſee—Martha Fulmer—Who is Martha Fulmer? Pſhaw! I won't be at the trouble of decyphering her damn'd pot-hooks. Hold, hold, hold; what have we got here!

"DEAR SIR,

"I've diſcover'd the lady you was ſo "much ſmitten with, and can procure you an interview "with her; if you can be as generous to a pretty girl as "you was to a paltry old captain," (how did ſhe find that out!) "you need not deſpair; come to me immediately; "the lady is now in my houſe, and expects you.

"Yours,

"MARTHA FULMER."

O thou dear, lovely, and enchanting paper, which I was about to tear into a thouſand ſcraps, devoutly I entreat thy pardon: I have ſlighted thy contents, which are delicious; ſlander'd thy characters, which are divine; and all the atonement I can make is implicitly to obey thy mandates.

STOCKWELL *returns.*

Stock. Mr. Belcour, here are the jewels; this letter encloſes bills for the money; and, if you will deliver it to Miſs Ruſport, you'll have no farther trouble on that ſcore.

Bel.

Bel. Ah, Sir! the letter which I've been reading difqualifies me for delivering the letter which you have been writing: I have other game on foot; the lovelieft girl my eyes ever feafted upon is ftarted in view, and the world cannot now divert me from purfuing her.

Stock. Hey-dey! What has turned you thus on a fudden?

Bel. A woman: one that can turn, and overturn me and my tottering refolutions every way fhe will. Oh, Sir, if this is folly in me, you muft rail at Nature: you muft chide the fun, that was vertical at my birth, and would not wink upon my nakednefs, but fwaddled me in the broadeft, hotteft glare of his meridian beams.

Stock. Mere rhapfody; mere childifh rhapfody; the libertine's familiar plea——Nature made us, 'tis true, but we are the refponfible creatures of our own faults and follies.

Bel. Sir!

Stock. Slave of every face you meet, fome huffey has inveigled you, fome handfome profligate, (the town is full of them;) and, when once fairly bankrupt in conftitution, as well as fortune, nature no longer ferves as your excufe for being vicious; neceffity, perhaps, will ftand your friend, and you'll reform.

Bel. You are fevere.

Stock It fits me to be fo—it well becomes a father——I would fay a friend—How ftrangely I forgot myfelf—How difficult it is to counterfeit indifference, and put a mafk upon the heart—I've ftruck him hard; he reddens.

Bel. How could you tempt me fo? Had you not inadvertently dropped the name of father, I fear our friendfhip, fhort as it has been, would fcarce have held me—But even your miftake I reverence—Give me your hand—'tis over.

Stock. Generous young man——let me embrace you——How fhall I hide my tears? I have been to blame; becaufe I bore you the affection of a father, I rafhly took up the authority of one. I afk your pardon—purfue your courfe; I have no right to ftop it——What would you have me do with thefe things?

Bel. This, if I might advife; carry the money to Mifs Rufport immediately; never let generofity wait for it's materials; that part of the bufinefs preffes. Give me the jewels; I'll find an opportunity of delivering them into her hands; and your vifit may pave the way for my reception. [*Exit.*

Stock. Be it fo: good morning to you. Farewel advice!

F Away

Away goes he upon the wing for pleaſure. What various paſſions he awakens in me! He pains, yet pleaſes me; affrights, offends, yet grows upon my heart. His very failings ſet him off—for ever treſpaſſing, for ever atoning, I almoſt think he would not be ſo perfect, were he free from fault: I muſt diſſemble longer; and yet how painful the experiment!—Even now he's gone upon ſome wild adventure; and who can tell what miſchief may befall him: O Nature, what it is to be a father! Juſt ſuch a thoughtleſs headlong thing was I when I beguiled his mother into love. [*Exit.*

SCENE II.

Scene changes to FULMER's *houſe.*

FULMER *and his* WIFE.

Ful. I tell you, Patty, you are a fool to think of bringing him and Miſs Dudley together; 'twill ruin every thing, and blow your whole ſcheme up to the moon at once.

Mrs. Ful. Why, ſure, Mr. Fulmer, I may be allowed to rear a chicken of my own hatching, as they ſay. Who firſt ſprung the thought but I, pray? Who firſt contrived the plot? Who propoſed the letter, but I, I?

Ful. And who dogg'd the gentleman home? Who found out his name, fortune, connection; that he was a Weſt-Indian, freſh landed, and full of caſh; a gull to our heart's content; a hot-brain'd headlong ſpark, that would run into our trap, like a wheat-ear under a turf?

Mrs. Ful. Hark! he's come: diſappear, march; and leave the field open to my machination. [*Exit* FULMER.

SCENE III.

BELCOUR *enters to her.*

Bel. O, thou dear miniſter to my happineſs, let me embrace thee! Why thou art my polar ſtar, my propitious conſtellation, by which I navigate my impatient bark into the port of pleaſure and delight.

Mrs. Ful. Oh, you men are ſly creatures! Do you remember now, you cruel, what you ſaid to me this morning?

Bel. All a jeſt, a frolick; never think on't; bury it for ever in oblivion; thou! why thou art all over nectar and ambroſia,

ambrosia, powder of pearl and odour of rof s; thou hast the youth of Hebe, the beauty of Venus, and the pen of Sappho; but in the name of all that's lovely, where's the lady! I expected to find her with you.

Mrs. Ful. No doubt you did, and these raptures were designed for her; but where have you loitered? the lady's gone, you are too late; girls of her sort are not to be kept waiting like negro slaves in your sugar plantations.

Bel. Gone! whither is she gone? tell me that I may follow her.

Mrs. Ful. Hold, hold, not so fast young gentleman, this is a case of some delicacy; shou'd Captain Dudley know that I introduced you to his daughter, he is a man of such scrupulous honour——

Bel. What do you tell me! is she daughter to the old gentleman I met here this morning?

Mrs. Ful. The same; him you was so generous to.

Bel. There's an end of the matter then at once; it shall never be said of me, that I took advantage of the father's necessities to trepan the daughter *(going.)*

Mrs. Ful. So, so, I've made a wrong cast, he's one of your conscientious sinners I find; but I won't lose him thus——Ha! ha! ha!

Bel. What is it you laugh at?

Mrs. Ful. Your absolute inexperience: have you lived so very little time in this country, as not to know that between young people of equal ages, the term of sister often is a cover for that of mistress? This young lady is, in that sense of the word, sister to young Dudley, and consequently daughter to my old lodger.

Bel. Indeed! are you serious?

Mrs. Ful. Can you doubt it? I must have been pretty well assur'd of that before I invited you hither.

Bel. That's true; she cannot be a woman of honour, and Dudley is an unconscionable young rogue to think of keeping one fine girl in pay, by raising contributions on another; he shall therefore give her up; she is a dear, bewitching, mischievous, little devil; and he shall positively give her up.

Mrs. Ful. Ay, now the freak has taken you again; I say give her up; there's one way, indeed, and certain of success.

Bel. What's that?

Mrs. Ful. Out-bid him, never dream of out-bluſtring him; buy out his leaſe of poſſeſſion, and leave her to manage his ejectment.

Bel. Is ſhe ſo venal? Never fear me then; when beauty is the purchaſe, I ſhan't think much of the price.

Mrs. Ful. All things, then, will be made eaſy enough; let me ſee; ſome little genteel preſent to begin with: what have you got about you? Ay, ſearch; I can beſtow it to advantage, there's no time to be loſt.

Bel. Hang it, conſound it; a plague upon't, ſay I! I hav'n't a guinea left in my pocket; I parted from my whole ſtock here this morning, and have forgot to ſupply myſelf ſince.

Mrs. Ful. Mighty well; let it paſs then; there's an end; think no more of the lady, that's all.

Bel. Diſtraction! think no more of her? let me only ſtep home and provide myſelf, I'll be back with you in an inſtant.

Mrs. Ful. Pooh, pooh! that's a wretched ſhift: have you nothing of value about you? Money's a coarſe ſlovenly vehicle, fit only to bribe electors in a borough; there are more graceful ways of purchaſing a lady's favours; rings, trinkets, jewels!

Bel. Jewels! Gadſo, I proteſt I had forgot: I have a caſe of jewels; but they won't do, I muſt not part from them: no, no, they are appropriated; they are none of my own.

Mrs. Ful. Let me ſee, let me ſee! Ay, now, this were ſomething-like: pretty creatures, how they ſparkle! theſe wou'd enſure ſucceſs.

Bel. Indeed!

Mrs. Ful. Theſe wou'd make her your own for ever.

Bel. Then the deuce take 'em for belonging to another perſon; I cou'd find in my heart to give 'em the girl, and ſwear I've loſt them.

Mrs. Ful. Ay, do, ſay they were ſtolen out of your pocket.

Bel. No, hang it, that's diſhonourable; here, give me the paltry things, I'll write you an order on my merchant for double their value.

Mrs. Ful. An order! No order for me! no orders upon merchants, with their value received, and three days grace; their noting, proteſting, and endorſing, and all their counting houſe formalities; I'll have nothing to do with them; leave

leave your diamonds with me, and give your order for the value of them to the owner: the money would be as good as the trinkets, I warrant you.

Bel. Hey! how! I never thought of that; but a breach of truſt; 'tis impoſſible; I never can conſent, therefore give me the jewels back again.

Mrs. Ful. Take 'em; I am now to tell you the lady is in this houſe?

Bel. In this houſe?

Mrs. Ful. Yes, Sir, in this very houſe; but what of that? you have got what you like better; your toys, your trinkets; go, go: Oh! you're a man of notable ſpirit, are you not?

Bel. Provoking creature! Bring me to the ſight of the dear girl, and diſpoſe of me as you think fit.

Mrs. Ful. And of the diamonds too?

Bel. Damn 'em, I wou'd there was not ſuch a bauble in nature! But come, come, diſpatch; if I had the throne of Dehli I ſhould give it to her.

Mrs. Ful. Swear to me then that you will keep within bounds, remember ſhe paſſes for the ſiſter of young Dudley. Oh! if you come to your flights, and your rhapſodies, ſhe'll be off in an inſtant.

Bel. Never fear me.

Mrs. Ful. You muſt expect to hear her talk of her father, as ſhe calls him, and her brother, and your bounty to her family.

Bel. Ay, ay, never mind what ſhe talks of, only bring her.

Mrs. Ful. You'll be prepar'd upon that head?

Bel. I ſhall be prepar'd, never fear; away with you.

Mrs. Ful. But hold, I had forgot: not a word of the diamonds; leave that matter to my management.

Bel. Hell and vexation! Get out of the room, or I ſhall run diſtracted. [*Exit Mrs. Fulmer.*] Of a certain, Belcour, thou art born to be the fool of woman: ſure no man ſins with ſo much repentance, or repents with ſo little amendment, as I do. I cannot give away another perſon's property, honour forbids me; and I poſitively cannot give up the girl: love, paſſion, conſtitution, every thing proteſts againſt that. How ſhall I decide? I cannot bring myſelf to break a truſt, and I am not at preſent in the humour to baulk my inclinations. Is there no middle way? Let me

conſider——

consider—There is, there is: my good genius has presented me with one; apt, obvious, honourable: the girl shall not go without her baubles, I'll not go without the girl, Miss Rusport shan't lose her diamonds, I'll save Dudley from destruction, and every party shall be a gainer by the project.

SCENE IV.

MRS. FULMER *introducing* MISS DUDLEY.

Mrs. Ful. Miss Dudley, this is the worthy gentleman you wish to see; this is Mr. Belcour.

Louisa. As I live the very man that beset me in the streets! (*aside.*)

Bel. An angel, by this light! Oh I am gone past all retrieving! (*aside.*)

Louisa. Mrs. Fulmer, Sir, informs me you are the gentleman from whom my father has received such civilities.

Bel. Oh! never name 'em.

Louisa. Pardon me, Mr. Belcour, they must be both named and remember'd; and if my father was here——

Bel. I am much better pleased with his representative.

Louisa. That title is my brother's, Sir; I have no claim to it.

Bel. I believe it.

Louisa. But as neither he nor my father were fortunate enough to be at home, I cou'd not resist the opportunity—

Bel. Nor I neither, by my soul, Madam: let us improve it, therefore. I am in love with you to distraction; I was charmed at the first glance; I attempted to accost you; you fled; I follow'd; but was defeated of an interview; at length I have obtain'd one, and seize the opportunity of casting my person and my fortune at your feet.

Louisa. You astonish me! Are you in your senses, or do you make a jest of my misfortunes? Do you ground pretences on your generosity, or do you make a practice of this folly with every woman you meet?

Bel. Upon my life, no: as you are the handsomest woman I ever met, so you are the first to whom I ever made the like professions: as for my generosity, Madam, I must refer you on that score to this good lady, who I believe has something to offer in my behalf.

Louisa.

Louisa. Don't build upon that, Sir; I muſt have better proofs of your generoſity, than the mere diveſtment of a little ſuperfluous droſs, before I an credit the ſincerity of profeſſions ſo abruptly delivered. [*Exit haſtily.*

Bel. Oh! ye Gods and Goddeſſes, how her anger animates her beauty! [*Going out.*

Mrs. Ful Stay, Sir; if you ſtir a ſtep after her, I renounce your intereſt for ever; why you'll ruin every thing.

Bel. Well, I muſt have her, coſt what it will: I ſee ſhe underſtands her own value tho'; a little ſuperfluous droſs, truly! She muſt have better proofs of my generoſity.

Mrs. Ful. 'Tis exactly as I told you; your money ſhe calls droſs; ſhe's too proud to ſtain her fingers with your coin; bait your hook well with jewels; try that experiment, and ſhe's your own.

Bel. Take 'em; let 'em go; lay 'em at her feet; I muſt get out of the ſcrape as I can; my propenſity is irreſiſtible: there; you have 'em; they are yours; they are hers; but remember they are a truſt; I commit them to her keeping till I can buy 'em off with ſomething ſhe ſhall think more valuable; now tell me when ſhall I meet her?

Mrs. Ful. How can I tell that? Don't you ſee what an alarm you have put her into? Oh! you're a rare one! But go your ways for this while; leave her to my management, and come to me at ſeven this evening; but remember not to bring empty pockets with you——Ha! ha! ah! [*Exeunt ſeverally.*

SCENE V.

LADY RUSPORT's *houſe.*

MISS RUSPORT *enters, followed by a Servant.*

Char. Deſire Mr. Stockwell to walk in. [*Exit Servant.*

STOCKWELL *enters.*

Stock. Madam, your moſt obedient ſervant: I am honoured with your commands, by Captain Dudley; and have brought the money with me as you directed; I underſtand the ſum you have occaſion for is two hundred pounds.

Char. It is, Sir; I am quite confounded at your taking this trouble upon yourſelf, Mr. Stockwell.

Stock.

Stock. There is a Bank-note, Madam, to the amount: your jewels are in safe hands, and will be delivered to you directly. If I had been happy in being better known to you, I should have hoped you would not have thought it necessary to place a deposit in my hands for so trifling a sum as you have now required me to supply you with.

Char. The baubles I sent you may very well be spared; and, as they are the only security in my present situation, I can give you, I could wish you would retain them in your hands: when I am of age, (which, if I live a few months, I shall be) I will replace your favour, with thanks.

Stock. It is obvious, Miss Rusport, that your charms will suffer no impeachment by the absence of those superficial ornaments; but they should be seen in the suite of a woman of fashion, not as creditors to whom you are indebted for your appearance, but as subservient attendants, which help to make up your equipage.

Char. Mr. Stockwell is determined not to wrong the confidence I reposed in his politeness.

Stock. I have only to request, Madam, that you will allow Mr. Belcour, a young gentleman, in whose happiness I particularly interest myself, to have the honour of delivering you the box of jewels.

Char. Most gladly; any friend of yours cannot fail of being welcome here.

Stock. I flatter myself you will not find him totally undeserving your good opinion; an education not of the strictest kind, and strong animal spirits, are apt sometimes to betray him into youthful irregularities; but an high principle of honour, and an uncommon benevolence, in the eye of candour, will, I hope, atone for any faults, by which these good qualities are not impaired.

Char. I dare say Mr. Belcour's behaviour wants no apology: we've no right to be over strict in canvassing the morals of a common acquaintance.

Stock. I wish it may be my happiness to see Mr. Belcour in the list, not of your common, but particular acquaintance, of your friends, Miss Rusport—I dare not be more explicit.

Char. Nor need you, Mr. Stockwell: I shall be studious to deserve his friendship; and, though I have long since unalterably placed my affections on another, I trust, I have not left myself insensible to the merits of Mr. Belcour;

and

and hope that neither you nor he will, for that reaſon, think me leſs worthy your good opinion and regards.

Stock. Miſs Ruſport, I ſincerely wiſh you happy: I have no doubt you have placed your affection on a deſerving man; and I have no right to combat your choice. [*Exit.*

Char. How honourable is that behaviour! Now, if Charles was here, I ſhould be happy. The old lady is ſo fond of her new Iriſh acquaintance, that I have the whole houſe at my diſpoſal. [*Exit* CHARLOTTE.

SCENE VI.

BELCOUR *enters, preceded by a* SERVANT.

Ser. I aſk your honour's pardon; I thought my young lady was here: who ſhall I inform her wou'd ſpeak to her?

Bel. Belcour is my name, Sir; and pray beg your lady to put herſelf in no hurry on my account; for I'd ſooner ſee the devil than ſee her face. (*Exit Servant.*) In the name of all that's miſchievous, why did Stockwell drive me hither in ſuch haſte? A pretty figure, truly, I ſhall make: an ambaſſador without credentials. Blockhead that I was to charge myſelf with her diamonds; officious, meddling puppy! Now they are irretrievably gone: that ſuſpicious jade Fulmer woudn't part even with a ſight of them, tho' I would have ranſom'd 'em at twice their value. Now muſt I truſt to my poor wits to bring me off: a lamentable dependance. Fortune be my helper: Here comes the girl— If ſhe is noble minded, as ſhe is ſaid to be, ſhe will forgive me; if not, 'tis a loſt cauſe; for I have not thought of one word in my excuſe.

SCENE VII.

CHARLOTTE *enters.*

Char. Mr. Belcour, I'm proud to ſee you: your friend, Mr. Stockwell, prepared me to expect this honour; and I am happy in the opportunity of being known to you.

Bel. A fine girl, by my ſoul! Now what a curſed hang-dog do I look like! (*aſide.*)

Char. You are newly arrived in this country, Sir?

Bel. Juſt landed, Madam; juſt ſet a ſhore, with a large cargo of Muſcavado ſugars, rum-puncheons, mahogany-ſlabs, wet ſweet-meats, and green paroquets.

 Char.

Char. May I aſk you how you like London, Sir?

Bel. To admiration: I think the town and the town'ſ-folk are exactly ſuited; 'tis a great, rich, overgrown, noiſy, tumultuous place: the whole morning is a buſtle to get money, and the whole afternoon is a hurry to ſpend it.

Char. Are theſe all the obſervations you have made?

Bel. No, Madam; I have obſerved the women are very captivating, and the men very ſoon caught.

Char. Ay, indeed! Whence do you draw that concluſion?

Bel. From infallible guides; the firſt remark I collect from what I now ſee, the ſecond from what I now feel.

Char. Oh, the deuce take you! But to wave this ſubject; I believe, Sir, this was a viſit of buſineſs, not compliment; was it not?

Bel. Ay; now comes on my execution.

Char. You have ſome fooliſh trinkets of mine, Mr. Belcour; havn't you?

Bel. No, in truth; they are gone in ſearch of a trinket, ſtill more fooliſh than themſelves. (*aſide.*)

Char. Some diamonds I mean, Sir; Mr. Stockwell inform'd me you was charg'd with 'em.

Bel. Oh, yes, Madam; but I have the moſt treacherous memory in life—Here they are! Pray put them up; they're all right; you need not examine 'em. (*gives a box.*)

Char. Hey-day! right, Sir! Why theſe are not my diamonds; theſe are quite different; and, as it ſhould ſeem, of much greater value.

Bel. Upon my life I'm glad on't; for then I hope you value 'em more than your own.

Char. As a purchaſer I ſhould, but not as an owner; you miſtake; theſe belong to ſomebody elſe.

Bel. 'Tis yours, I'm afraid, that belong to ſomebody elſe.

Char. What is it you mean? I muſt inſiſt upon your taking 'em back again.

Bel. Pray, Madam, don't do that; I ſhall infallibly loſe them; I have the worſt luck with diamonds of any man living.

Char. That you might well ſay, was you to give me theſe in the place of mine; but pray, Sir, what is the reaſon of all this? Why have you changed the jewels? And where have you diſpoſed of mine?

Bel.

Bel. Miſs Ruſport, I cannot invent a lie for my life; and, if it was to ſave it, I coudn't tell one: I am an idle, diſſipated, unthinking fellow, not worth your notice: in ſhort, I am a Weſt Indian; and you muſt try me according to the charter of my colony, not by a jury of Engliſh ſpinſters: the truth is, I've given away your jewels; caught with a pair of ſparkling eyes, whoſe luſtre blinded their's, I ſerved your property as I ſhould my own, and laviſh'd it away; let me not totally deſpair of your forgiveneſs: I frequently do wrong, but never with impunity; if your diſpleaſure is added to my own, my puniſhment will be too ſevere. When I parted from the jewels, I had not the honour of knowing their owner.

Char. Mr. Belcour, your ſincerity charms me; I enter at once into your character, and I make all the allowances for it you can deſire. I take your jewels for the preſent, becauſe I know there is no other way of reconciling you to yourſelf; but, if I give way to your ſpirit in one point, you muſt yield to mine in another: remember I will not keep more than the value of my own jewels: there is no need to be pillaged by more than one woman at a time, Sir.

Bel. Now, may every bleſſing that can crown your virtues, and reward your beauty, be ſhower'd upon you; may you meet admiration without envy, love without jealouſy, and old age without malady; may the man of your heart be ever conſtant, and you never meet a leſs penitent, or leſs grateful offender, than myſelf!

(Servant enters and delivers a letter.)

Char. Does your letter require ſuch haſte?

Ser. I was bade to give it into your own hands, Madam.

Char. From Charles Dudley, I ſee—have I your permiſſion? Good Heaven, what do I read! Mr. Belcour, you are concern'd in this——" Dear Charlotte, in the " midſt of our diſtreſs, Providence has caſt a benefactor " in our way, after the moſt unexpected manner: a " young Weſt Indian, rich, and, with a warmth of " heart peculiar to his climate, has reſcued my father from " his troubles, ſatisfied his wants, and enabled him to ac" compliſh his exchange: when I relate to you the man" ner in which this was done, you will be charmed; I can " only now add, that it was by chance we found out that "his name is Belcour, and that he is a friend of Mr. "Stockwell's. I lose not a moment's time, in making you "acquainted with this fortunate event, for reasons which "delicacy obliges me to suppress; but, perhaps, if you "have not received the money on your jewels, you will "not think it necessary now to do it. I have the honour "to be,

"Dear Madam,

"most faithfully, yours,

"CHARLES DUDLEY."

Is this your doing, Sir? Never was generosity so worthily exerted.

Bel. Or so greatly overpaid.

Char. After what you have now done for this noble, but indigent family, let me not scruple to unfold the whole situation of my heart to you. Know then, Sir, (and don't think the worse of me for the frankness of my declaration) that such is my attachment to the son of that worthy officer, whom you relieved, that the moment I am of age, and in possession of my fortune, I shou'd hold myself the happiest of women to share it with young Dudley.

Bel. Say you so, Madam! then let me perish if I don't love and reverence you above all woman kind; and, if such is your generous resolution, never wait till you're of age; life is too short, pleasure too fugitive; the soul grows narrower every hour; I'll equip you for your escape; I'll convey you to the man of your heart, and away with you then to the first hospitable parson that will take you in.

Char. O blessed be the torrid zone for ever, whose rapid vegetation quickens nature into such benignity! These latitudes are made for politics and philosophy; friendship has no root in this soil. But, had I spirit to accept your offer, which is not improbable, woudn't it be a mortifying thing, for a fond girl to find herself mistaken, and sent back to her home, like a vagrant; and such, for what I know, might be my case.

Bel. Then he ought to be proscribed the society of mankind for ever——Ay, ay, 'tis the sham sister that makes him thus indifferent; 'twill be a meritorious office to take that girl out of the way.

SCENE

SCENE VIII.

(*Servant enters.*)

Ser. Miſs Dudley to wait on you, Madam.

Bel. Who?

Ser. Miſs Dudley.

Char. What's the matter, Mr. Belcour? Are you frighted at the name of a pretty girl! 'Tis the ſiſter of him we were ſpeaking of—pray admit her.

Bel. The ſiſter! So, ſo; he has impoſed on her too—this is an extraordinary viſit, truly. Upon my ſoul, the aſſurance of ſome folks is not to be accounted for.

Char. I inſiſt upon your not running away; you'll be charm'd with Louiſa Dudley.

Bel. Oh, yes, I am charmed with her.

Char. You've ſeen her then, have you?

Bel. Yes, yes, I've ſeen her.

Char. Well, isn't ſhe a delightful girl?

Bel. Very delightful.

Char. Why, you anſwer as if you was in a court of juſtice: O' my conſcience! I believe you are caught; I've a notion ſhe has trick'd you out of your heart.

Bel. I believe ſhe has, and you out of your jewels; for, to tell you the truth, ſhe's the very perſon I gave 'em to.

Char. You gave her my jewels! Louiſa Dudley my jewels? admirable! inimitable! Oh, the ſly little jade! but huſh, here ſhe comes; I don't know how I ſhall keep my countenance. (LOUISA *enters.*) My dear, I'm rejoiced to ſee you; how d'ye do? I beg leave to introduce Mr. Belcour, a very worthy friend of mine; I believe, Louiſa, you have ſeen him before.

Lou. I have met the gentleman.

Char. You have met the gentleman: well, Sir, and you have met the lady; in ſhort, you have met each other; why then don't you ſpeak to each other? How you both ſtand! tongue-tied, and fix'd as ſtatues——Ha! ha! ha! Why you'll fall aſleep by-and-by.

Lou. Fye upon you: fye upon you; is this fair?

Bel. Upon my ſoul, I never look'd ſo like a fool in my life; the aſſurance of that girl puts me quite down. (*aſide.*)

Char. Sir—Mr. Belcour—Was it your pleaſure to advance

vance any thing? Not a ſyllable. Come, Louiſa, women's wit, they ſay, is never at a loſs—Nor you neither? Speechleſs both—Why you was merry enough before this lady came in.

Lou. I am ſorry I have been any interruption to your happineſs, Sir.

Bel. Madam!

Char. Madam! Is that all you can ſay? But come, my dear girl, I won't teaze you: apropos! I muſt ſhew you what a preſent this dumb gentleman has made me: are not theſe handſome diamonds?

Lou. Yes, indeed, they ſeem very fine; but I am no judge of theſe things.

Char. Oh, you wicked little hypocrite, you are no judge of theſe things, Louiſa; you have no diamonds, not you.

Lou. You know I havn't, Miſs Ruſport. you know thoſe things are infinitely above my reach.

Char. Ha! ha! ha!

Bel. She does tell a lie with an admirable countenance, that's true enough.

Lou. What ails you, Charlotte? What impertinence have I been guilty of that you ſhould find it neceſſary to humble me at ſuch a rate? If you are happy, long may you be ſo; but, ſurely, it can be no addition to it to make me miſerable.

Char. So ſerious! there muſt be ſome myſtery in this—Mr. Belcour, will you leave us together? You ſee I treat you with all the familiarity of an old acquaintance already.

Bel. Oh, by all means, pray command me. Miſs Ruſport, I'm your moſt obedient! By your condeſcenſion in accepting theſe poor trifles, I am under eternal obligations to you—To you, Miſs Dudley, I ſhall not offer a word on that ſubject: you deſpiſe finery; you have a ſoul above it; I adore your ſpirit; I was rather unprepared for meeting you here; but I ſhall hope for an opportunity of making myſelf better known to you. [*Exit.*

SCENE IX.

CHARLOTTE *and* LOUISA.

Char. Louiſa Dudley, you ſurprize me; I never ſaw you act thus before: can't you bear a little innocent raillery before the man of your heart?

Lou.

Lou. The man of my heart, Madam? Be aſſured I never was ſo viſionary to aſpire to any man whom Miſs Ruſport honours with her choice.

Char. My choice, my dear! Why we are playing at croſs purpoſes: how enter'd it into your head that Mr. Belcour was the man of my choice?

Lou. Why, didn't he preſent you with thoſe diamonds?

Char. Well; perhaps he did—and pray, Louiſa, have you no diamonds?

Lou. I diamonds truly! Who ſhould give me diamonds?

Char. Who, but this very gentleman: apropos! here comes your brother———

SCENE X.

(CHARLES *enters.*)

I inſiſt upon referring our diſpute to him: your ſiſter and I, Charles, have a quarrel; Belcour, the hero of your letter, has juſt left us—ſome how or other, Louiſa's bright eyes have caught him; and the poor fellow's fallen deſperately in love with her—(don't interrupt me, huſſey)—Well, that's excuſable enough, you'll ſay; but the jet of the ſtory is, that this hair-brain'd ſpark, who does nothing like other people, has given her the very identical jewels, which you pledged for me to Mr. Stockwell; and will you believe that this little demure ſlut made up a face, and ſqueezed out three or four hypocritical tears, becauſe I rallied her about it.

Charles. I'm all aſtoniſhment! Louiſa, tell me without reſerve, has Mr. Belcour given you any diamonds?

Lou. None, upon my honour.

Charles. Has he made any profeſſions to you?

Lou. He has; but altogether in a ſtile ſo whimſical and capricious, that the beſt which can be ſaid of them is to tell you, that they ſeem'd more the reſult of good ſpirits than good manners.

Char. Ay, ay, now the murder's out; he's in love with her, and ſhe has no very great diſlike to him; truſt to my obſervation, Charles, for that: as to the diamonds, there's ſome miſtake about them, and you muſt clear it up: three minutes converſation with him will put every thing

in

in a right train; go, go, Charles, 'tis a brother's bufinefs; about it inftantly; ten to one you'll find him over the way at Mr. Stockwell's.

Charles. I confefs, I'm impatient to have the cafe clear'd up; I'll take your advice, and find him out, good bye to you.

Char. Your fervant; my life upon it you'll find Belcour a man of honour. Come, Louifa, let us adjourn to my dreffing-room; I've a little private bufinefs to tranfact with you, before the old lady comes up to tea, and interrupts us.

END OF THE THIRD ACT.

ACT

ACT IV. SCENE I.

FULMER's *house*.

FULMER *and* MRS. FULMER.

Ful. PATTY, wasn't Mr. Belcour with you?

Mrs. Ful. He was; and is now ſhut up in my chamber, in high expectation of an interview with Miſs Dudley; ſhe's at preſent with her brother, and 'twas with ſome difficulty I perſuaded my hot-headed ſpark to wait till he has left her.

Ful. Well, child, and what then?

Mrs. Ful. Why then, Mr. Fulmer, I think it will be time for you and me to ſteal a march, and be gone.

Ful. So this is all the fruit of your ingenious project; a ſhameful overthrow, or a ſudden flight.

Mrs. Ful. Why, my project was a mere impromptu, and can at worſt but quicken our departure a few days; you know we had fairly outliv'd our credit here, and a trip to Boulogne is no ways unſeaſonable. Nay, never droop, man—Hark! hark! here's enough to bear charges (*ſhewing a purſe.*)

Ful. Let me ſee, let me ſee: this weighs well; this is of the right ſort: why your Weſt-Indian bled freely.

Mrs. Ful. But that's not all: look here! Here are the ſparklers! (*ſhewing the jewels*) Now what d'ye think of my performances? Heh! a fooliſh ſcheme, isn't it—a ſilly woman—?

Ful. Thou art a Judith, a Joan of Arc, and I'll march under thy banners, girl, to the world's end: come, let's begone; I've little to regret; my creditors may ſhare the old books amongſt them; they'll have occaſion for philoſophy to ſupport their loſs; they'll find enough upon my ſhelves: the world is my library; I read mankind—Now, Patty, lead the way.

Mrs. Ful. Adieu, Belcour! [*Exeunt.*

SCENE II.

CHARLES DUDLEY *and* LOUISA.

Charles. Well, Louiſa, I confeſs the force of what you ſay: I accept Miſs Ruſport's bounty; and, when you ſee my generous Charlotte, tell her——but have a care, there is a ſelfiſhneſs even in gratitude, when it is too profuſe; to be overthankful for any one favour, is in effect to lay out for another; the beſt return I cou'd make my benefactreſs wou'd be never to ſee her more.

Lou. I underſtand you.

Charles. We that are poor, Louiſa, ſhou'd be cautious: for this reaſon, I wou'd guard you againſt Belcour; at leaſt till I can unravel the myſtery of Miſs Ruſport's diamonds; I was diſappointed of finding him at Mr. Stockwell's, and am now going in ſearch of him again: he may intend honourably; but, I confeſs to you, I am ſtagger'd; think no more of him, therefore, for the preſent: of this be ſure, while I have life, and you have honour, I will protect you, or periſh in your defence. [*Exit.*

Lou. Think of him no more! Well, I'll obey; but if a wand'ring uninvited thought ſhould creep by chance into my boſom, muſt not I give the harmleſs wretch a ſhelter? Oh! yes; the great artificer of the human heart knows every thread he wove into its fabric, nor puts his work to harder uſes than it was made to bear: my wiſhes then, my guiltleſs ones, I mean, are free: how faſt they ſpring within me at that ſentence! Down, down, ye buſy creatures! Whither wou'd you carry me? Ah! there is one amongſt you, a forward, new intruder, that, in the likeneſs of an offending, generous, man, grows into favour with my heart. Fye, fye upon it! Belcour purſues, inſults me; yet, ſuch is the fatality of my condition, that what ſhou'd rouſe reſentment, only calls up love.

SCENE III.

(BELCOUR *enters to her.*)

Bel. Alone, by all that's happy!

Lou. Ah!

Bel. Oh! ſhriek not, ſtart not, ſtir not, lovelieſt creature! but let me kneel, and gaze upon your beauties.

Lou. Sir! Mr. Belcour, riſe! What is it you do?

Bel. See, I obey you; mould me as you will, behold your ready ſervant! New to your country, ignorant of your manners, habits, and deſires, I put myſelf into your hands for inſtruction; make me only ſuch as you can like yourſelf, and I ſhall be happy.

Lou. I muſt not hear this, Mr. Belcour; go; ſhould

he

he that parted from me but this minute, now return, I tremble for the conſequence.

Bel. Fear nothing; let him come: I love you, Madam; he'll find it hard to make me unſay that.

Louiſa. You terrify me; your impetuous temper frightens me; you know my ſituation; it is not generous to purſue me thus.

Bel. True; I do know your ſituation, your real one, Miſs Dudley, and am reſolv'd to ſnatch you from it; 'twill be a meritorious act; the old Captain ſhall rejoice; Miſs Ruſport ſhall be made happy: and even he, even your beloved brother, with whoſe reſentment you threaten me, ſhall in the end applaud and thank me: Come, thou'rt a dear enchanting girl, and I'm determin'd not to live a minute longer without thee.

Louiſa. Hold, are you mad? I ſee you are a bold aſſuming man, and know not where to ſtop.

Bel. Who that beholds ſuch beauty can? By Heaven, you put my blood into a flame. Provoking girl! is it within the ſtretch of my fortune to content you? What is it you can further aſk that I am not ready to grant?

Louiſa. Yes, with the ſame facility that you beſtow'd upon me Miſs Ruſport's diamonds. For ſhame! for ſhame! was that a manly ſtory?

Bel. So! ſo! theſe deviliſh diamonds meet me every where—Let me periſh if I mean't you any harm: Oh! I cou'd tear my tongue out for ſaying a word about the matter.

Louiſa. Go to her then and contradict it; till that is done, my reputation is at ſtake.

Bel. Her reputation! Now ſhe has got upon that, ſhe'll go on for ever.—What is there I will not do for your ſake? I will go to Miſs Ruſport.

Louiſa. Do ſo; reſtore her own jewels to her, which I ſuppoſe you kept back for the purpoſe of preſenting others to her of a greater value; but for the future, Mr. Belcour, when you wou'd do a gallant action to that lady, don't let it be at my expence.

Bel. I ſee where ſhe points: ſhe is willing enough to give up Miſs Ruſport's diamonds, now ſhe finds ſhe ſhall be a gainer by the exchange. Be it ſo! 'tis what I wiſh'd.—Well, Madam, I will return to Miſs Ruſport her own jewels, and you ſhall have others of tenfold their value.

Louiſa. No, Sir, you err moſt widely; it is my good opinion, not my vanity, which you muſt bribe.

Bel. Why, what the devil wou'd ſhe have now?—Miſs Dudley, it is my wiſh to obey and pleaſe you, but I have ſome apprehenſion that we miſtake each other.

Louiſa. I think we do: tell me, then, in few words, what it is you aim at.

Bel. In few words, then, and in plain honeſty, I muſt tell you, ſo entirely am I captivated with you, that had you but been ſuch as it would have become me to have call'd my wife, I had been happy in knowing you by that name; as it is, you are welcome to partake my fortune, give me in return your perſon, give me pleaſure, give me love; free, diſencumber'd, antimatrimonial love.

Louiſa. Stand off, and let me never ſee you more.

Bel. Hold, hold, thou dear, tormenting, tantalizing girl! Upon my knees I ſwear you ſhall not ſtir till you've conſented to my bliſs.

Louiſa. Unhand me, Sir: O Charles! protect me, reſcue me, redreſs me. [*Exit.*

SCENE IV.

CHARLES DUDLEY *enters.*

Charles. How's this! Riſe, villain, and defend yourſelf.

Bel. Villain!

Charles. The man who wrongs that lady is a villain—Draw!

Bel. Never fear me, young gentleman; brand me for a coward, if I baulk you.

Charles. Yet hold! Let me not be too haſty: your name I think, is Belcour.

Bel. Well, Sir.

Charles. How is it, Mr. Belcour, you have done this mean, unmanly wrong; beneath the maſk of generoſity to give this fatal ſtab to our domeſtic peace? You might have had my thanks, my bleſſing; take my defiance now. 'Tis Dudley ſpeaks to you, the brother, the protector of that injur'd lady.

Bel. The brother? Give yourſelf a truer title.

Charles. What is't you mean?

Bel.

Bel. Come, come, I know both her and you: I found you, Sir, (but how or why I know not) in the good graces of Miſs Ruſport—(yes, colour at that name!) I gave you no diſturbance there, never broke in upon you in that rich and plenteous quarter, but, when I cou'd have blaſted all your projects with a word, ſpar'd you, in fooliſh pity ſpar'd you, nor rouz'd her from the fond credulity in which your artifice had lull'd her.

Charles. No, Sir, nor boaſted to her of the ſplendid preſent you had made my poor Louiſa; the diamonds, Mr. Belcour; how was that? What can you plead to that arraignment?

Bel. You queſtion me too late; the name of Belcour and of villain never met before; had you enquir'd of me before you utter'd that raſh word, you might have ſav'd yourſelf or me a mortal error: now, Sir, I neither give nor take an explanation; ſo, come on! [*They fight.*

SCENE V.

LOUISA, *and afterwards* O'FLAHERTY.

Louiſa, Hold, hold, for Heaven's ſake hold! Charles!— Mr. Belcour! Help! Sir, Sir, make haſte, they'll murder one another.

O'Fla. Hell and confuſion! What's all this uproar for? Can't you leave off cutting one another's throats, and mind what the poor girl ſays to you? You've done a notable thing, hav'n't you both, to put her into ſuch a flurry? I think, o' my conſcience, ſhe's the moſt frighted of the three.

Charles. Dear Louiſa, recollect yourſelf; why did you interfere? 'Tis in your cauſe.

Bel. Now cou'd I kill him for careſſing her.

O'Fla. O Sir, your moſt obedient! You are the gentleman I had the honour of meeting here before; you was then running off at full ſpeed like a Calmuck, now you are tilting and driving like a bedlamite with this lad here, that ſeems as mad as yourſelf: 'Tis pity but your country had a little more employment for you both.

Bel. Mr. Dudley, when you've recover'd the lady, you know where I am to be found. [*Exit.*

O'Fla. Well then, can't you ſtay where you are, and that will ſave the trouble of looking after you? Yon volatile

latile fellow thinks to give a man the meeting by getting out of his way: by my ſoul 'tis a round-about method that of his. But I think he call'd you Dudley: Hark'e, young man, are you ſon of my friend the old captain?

Charles. I am. Help me to convey this lady to her chamber, and I ſhall be more at leiſure to anſwer your queſtions.

O'Fla. Ay will I: come along, pretty one; if you've had wrong done you, young man, you need look no further for a ſecond; Dennis O'Flaherty's your man for that: but never draw your ſword before a woman, Dudley; damn it, never while you live draw your ſword before a woman. [*Exeunt.*

SCENE VI.

LADY RUSPORT'S HOUSE.

LADY RUSPORT *and* SERVANT.

Ser. An elderly gentleman, who ſays his name is Varland, deſires leave to wait on your ladyſhip.

L. Ruſ. Shew him in; the very man I wiſh to ſee: Varland, he was Sir Oliver's ſolicitor, and privy to all his affairs; he brings ſome good tidings; ſome freſh mortgage, or another bond come to light, they ſtart up every day. (VARLAND *enters.*) Mr. Varland, I'm glad to ſee you; you're heartily welcome, honeſt Mr. Varland; you and I havn't met ſince our late irreparable loſs: how have you paſſed your time this age?

Var. Truly, my lady, ill enough: I thought I muſt have followed good Sir Oliver.

L. Ruſ. Alack-a-day, poor man! Well, Mr. Varland, you find me here overwhelmed with trouble and fatigue; torn to pieces with a multiplicity of affairs; a great fortune poured upon me unſought for and unexpected: 'twas my good father's will and pleaſure it ſhould be ſo, and I muſt ſubmit.

Var. Your ladyſhip inherits under a will made in the year forty-five, immediately after Captain Dudley's marriage with your ſiſter.

L. Ruſ. I do ſo, Mr. Varland; I do ſo.

Var. I well remember it; I engroſſed every ſyllable; but I am ſurprized to find your ladyſhip ſet ſo little ſtore by this vaſt acceſſion.

L. Ruſ.

L. Ruſ. Why you know, Mr. Varland, I am a moderate woman; I had enough before; a ſmall matter ſatisfies me; and Sir Stephen Ruſport (Heaven be his portion!) took care I ſhoudn't want that.

Var. Very true; very true, he did ſo; and I am overjoyed at finding your ladyſhip in this diſpoſition; for, truth to ſay, I was not without apprehenſion the news I have to communicate would have been of ſome prejudice to your ladyſhip's tranquillity.

L. Ruſ. News, Sir! What news have you for me?

Var. Nay, nothing to alarm you; a trifle, in your preſent way of thinking: I have a will of Sir Oliver's you have never ſeen.

L. Ruſ. A will! Impoſſible! How came you by it, pray?

Var. I drew it up, at his command, in his laſt illneſs: it will ſave you a world of trouble: it gives his whole eſtate from you to his grandſon, Charles Dudley.

L. Ruſ. To Dudley? His eſtate to Charles Dudley? I can't ſupport it! I ſhall faint! You've killed me, you vile man! I never ſhall ſurvive it!

Var. Look'e there now: I proteſt, I thought you would have rejoiced at being clear of the incumbrance.

L. Ruſ. 'Tis falſe; 'tis all a forgery, concerted between you and Dudley; why elſe did I never hear of it before?

Var. Have patience, my lady, and I'll tell you: By Sir Oliver's direction, I was to deliver this will into no hands but his grandſon Dudley's: the young gentleman happen'd to be then in Scotland; I was diſpatch'd thither in ſearch of him: the hurry and fatigue of my journey brought on a fever by the way, which confined me in extreme danger for ſeveral days; upon my recovery, I purſued my journey, found young Dudley had left Scotland in the interim, and am now directed hither; where, as ſoon I can find him, doubtleſs, I ſhall diſcharge my conſcience, and fulfil my commiſſion.

L. Ruſ. Dudley then, as yet, knows nothing of this will?

Var. Nothing; that ſecret reſts with me.

L. Ruſ. A thought occurs: by this fellow's talking of his conſcience, I ſhould gueſs it was upon ſale. (*aſide.*) Come, Mr. Varland, if 'tis as you ſay, I muſt ſubmit. I was ſomewhat flurried at firſt, and forgot myſelf; I aſk

your

your pardon: this is no place to talk of busineſs; ſtep with me into my room; we will there compare the will, and reſolve accordingly——Oh! would your fever had you, and I had your paper. [*Exeunt.*

SCENE VII.

MISS RUSPORT, CHARLES, *and* O'FLAHERTY.

Char. So, ſo! My lady and her lawyer have retired to cloſe confabulation: now, Major, if you are the generous man I take you for, grant me one favour.

O'Fla. Faith will I, and not think much of my generoſity neither; for, though it may not be in my power to do the favour you aſk, look you, it can never be in my heart to refuſe it.

Charles. Cou'd this man's tongue do juſtice to his thoughts, how eloquent would he be! (*aſide.*)

Char. Plant yourſelf then in that room: keep guard, for a few moments, upon the enemy's motions, in the chamber beyond; and, if they ſhould attempt a ſally, ſtop their march a moment, till your friend here can make good his retreat down the back-ſtairs.

O'Fla. A word to the wiſe! I'm an old campaigner; make the beſt uſe of your time; and truſt me for tying the old cat up to the picket.

Char. Huſh! huſh! not ſo loud.

Charles. 'Tis the office of a centinel, Major, you have undertaken, rather than that of a field-officer.

O'Fla. 'Tis the office of a friend, my dear boy; and therefore, no diſgrace to a general. [*Exit.*

SCENE VIII.

CHARLES *and* CHARLOTTE.

Char. Well, Charles, will you commit yourſelf to me for a few minutes?

Charles. Moſt readily; and let me, before one goes by, tender you the only payment I can ever make for your abundant generoſity.

Char. Hold, hold! ſo vile a thing as money muſt not come between us. What ſhall I ſay! O Charles! O Dudley! What difficulties have you thrown upon me!

Familiarly

Familiarly as we have lived, I ſhrink not at what I'm doing; and, anxiouſly as I have ſought this opportunity, my fears almoſt perſuade me to abandon it.

Charles. You alarm me!

Char. Your looks and actions have been ſo diſtant, and at this moment are ſo deterring, that, was it not for the hope that delicacy, and not diſguſt, inſpires this conduct in you, I ſhould ſink with ſhame and apprehenſion; but time preſſes; and I muſt ſpeak; and plainly too—Was you now in poſſeſſion of your grandfather's eſtate, as juſtly you ought to be; and, was you inclined to ſeek a companion for life, ſhould you, or ſhould you not, in that caſe, honour your unworthy Charlotte with your choice?

Charles. My unworthy Charlotte! So judge me Heaven, there is not a circumſtance on earth ſo valuable as your happineſs, ſo dear to me as your perſon; but to bring poverty, diſgrace, reproach from friends, ridicule from all the world, upon a generous benefactreſs; thieviſhly to ſteal into an open, unreſerved, ingenuous heart, O Charlotte! dear, unhappy girl, it is not to be done.

Char. Nay, now you rate too highly the poor advantages fortune alone has given me over you: how otherwiſe could we bring our merits to any balance? Come, my dear Charles, I have enough; make that enough ſtill more, by ſharing it with me: ſole heireſs of my father's fortune, a ſhort time will put it in my diſpoſal; in the mean while you will be ſent to join your regiment; let us prevent a ſeparation, by ſetting out this very night for that happy country where marriage ſtill is free: carry me this moment to Belcour's lodgings.

Charles. Belcour's?—The name is ominous; there's murder in it: bloody inexorable honour! (*aſide.*)

Char. D'ye pauſe? Put me into his hands, while you provide the means for our eſcape: he is the moſt generous, the moſt honourable of men.

Charles. Honourable! moſt honourable!

Char. Can you doubt it? Do you demur? Have you forgot your letter? Why, Belcour 'twas that prompted me to this propoſal, that promiſed to ſupply the means, that nobly offer'd his unaſk'd aſſiſtance——

(O'Flaherty *enters haſtily.*)

O'Fla. Run, run, for holy St. Antony's ſake, to horſe

and away! The conference is broke up, and the old lady advances upon a full Piedmontese trot, within pistol-shot of your encampment.

Char. Here, here, down the back-stairs! O Charles, remember me!

Charles. Farewell! Now, now I feel myself a coward. [*Exit.*

Char. What does he mean?

O'Fla. Ask no questions, but be gone: she has cooled the lad's courage, and wonders he feels like a coward. There's a damn'd deal of mischief brewing between this hyena and her lawyer: egad I'll step behind this screen and listen: a good soldier must sometimes fight in ambush as well as open field. (*retires.*)

SCENE IX.

LADY RUSPORT *and* VARLAND.

L. Rus. Sure I heard somebody. Hark! No; only the servants going down the back-stairs. Well, Mr. Varland, I think then we are agreed: you'll take my money; and your conscience no longer stands in your way.

Var. Your father was my benefactor; his will ought to be sacred; but, if I commit it to the flames, how will he be the wiser? Dudley, 'tis true, has done me no harm; but five thousand pounds will do me much good; so, in short, Madam, I take your offer; I will confer with my clerk, who witnessed the will; and to-morrow morning put it into your hands, upon condition you put five thousand good pounds into mine.

L. Rus. 'Tis a bargain: I'll be ready for you: farewell. [*Exit.*

Var. Let me consider—Five thousand pounds prompt payment for destroying this scrap of paper, not worth five farthings; 'tis a fortune easily earn'd; yes; and 'tis another man's fortune easily thrown away: 'tis a good round sum to be paid down at once for a bribe; but 'tis a damn'd rogue's trick in me to take it.

O'Fla. So, so! this fellow speaks truth to himself, tho' he lies to other people—but hush! (*aside.*)

Var. 'Tis breaking the trust of my benefactor; that's a foul crime; but he's dead, and can never reproach me with it: and 'tis robbing young Dudley of his lawful patrimony;

trimony; that's a hard caſe; but he's alive, and knows nothing of the matter.

O'Fla. Theſe lawyers are ſo uſed to bring off the rogueries of others, that they are never without an excuſe for their own. (*aſide.*)

Var. Were I aſſured now that Dudley would give me half the money for producing this will, that Lady Ruſport does for concealing it, I would deal with him, and be an honeſt man at half price; I wiſh every gentleman of my profeſſion could lay his hand on his heart and ſay the ſame thing.

O'Fla. A bargain, old gentleman! Nay, never ſtart, nor ſtare, you waſn't afraid of your own conſcience, never be afraid of me.

Var. Of you, Sir; who are you, pray?

O'Fla. I'll tell you who I am: you ſeem to wiſh to be honeſt, but want the heart to ſet about it; now I am the very man in the world to make you ſo; for, if you do not give me up that paper this very inſtant, by the ſoul of me, fellow, I will not leave one whole bone in your ſkin that ſhan't be broken.

Var. What right have you, pray, to take this paper from me?

O'Fla. What right have you, pray, to keep it from young Dudley? I don't know what it contains, but I am apt to think it will be ſafer in my hands than in your's; therefore give it me without more words, and ſave yourſelf a beating: do now; you had beſt.

Var. Well, Sir, I may as well make a grace of neceſſity. There; I have acquitted my conſcience, at the expence of five thouſand pounds.

O'Fla. Five thouſand pounds! Mercy upon me! When there are ſuch temptations in the law, can we wonder if ſome of the corps are a diſgrace to it?

Var. Well, you have got the paper; if you are an honeſt man, give it to Charles Dudley.

O'Fla. An honeſt man! look at me, friend, I am a ſoldier, this is not the livery of a knave; I am an Iriſhman, honey; mine is not the country of diſhonour. Now, ſirrah, be gone; if you enter theſe doors, or give Lady Ruſport the leaſt item of what has paſſed, I will cut off both your ears, and rob the pillory of its due.

Var. I wiſh I was once fairly out of his ſight. [*Exeunt.*

SCENE X.

A Room in STOCKWELL'*s House.*

Stock. I must disclose myself to Belcour; this noble instance of his generosity, which old Dudley has been relating, allies me to him at once; concealment becomes too painful; I shall be proud to own him for my son——But see, he's here.

(BELCOUR *enters, and throws himself upon a sopha.*)

Bel. O my curst tropical constitution! Wou'd to Heaven I had been dropt upon the snows of Lapland, and never felt the blessed influence of the sun, so I had never burnt with these inflammatory passions!

Stock. So, so, you seem disorder'd, Mr. Belcour.

Bel. Disorder'd, Sir! Why did I ever quit the soil in which I grew; what evil planet drew me from that warm sunny region, where naked Nature walks without disguise, into this cold contriving artificial country?

Stock. Come, Sir, you've met a rascal; what o'that? general conclusions are illiberal.

Bel. No, Sir, I've met reflection by the way; I've come from folly, noise, and fury, and met a silent monitor—Well, well, a villain! 'twas not to be pardon'd—pray never mind me, Sir.

Stock. Alas! my heart bleeds for him.

Bel. And yet, I might have heard him: now, plague upon that blundering Irishman for coming in as he did; the hurry of the deed might palliate the event: deliberate execution has less to plead—Mr. Stockwell, I am bad company to you.

Stock. Oh, Sir; make no excuse. I think you have not found me forward to pry into the secrets of your pleasures and pursuits; 'tis not my disposition; but there are times, when want of curiosity wou'd be want of friendship.

Bel. Ah, Sir, mine is a case wherein you and I shall never think alike; the punctilious rules, by which I am bound, are not to be found in your ledgers, nor will pass current in the compting-house of a trader.

Stock. 'Tis very well, Sir; if you think I can render you any service, it may be worth your trial to confide in me; if not, your secret is safer in your own bosom.

Bel.

Bel. That ſentiment demands my confidence: pray, ſit down by me. You muſt know, I have an affair of honour on my hands with young Dudley; and, tho' I put up with no man's inſult, yet I wiſh to take away no man's life.

Stock. I know the young man, and am appris'd of your generoſity to his father; what can have bred a quarrel between you?

Bel. A fooliſh paſſion on my ſide, and a haughty provocation on his. There is a girl, Mr. Stockwell, whom I have unfortunately ſeen, of moſt uncommon beauty; ſhe has withal an air of ſo much natural modeſty, that had I not had good aſſurance of her being an attainable wanton, I declare I ſhou'd as ſoon have thought of attempting the chaſtity of Diana.

SERVANT *enters.*

Stock. Hey-dey, do you interrupt us?

Ser. Sir, there's an Iriſh gentleman will take no denial; he ſays he muſt ſee Mr. Belcour directly, upon buſineſs of the laſt conſequence.

Bel. Admit him; 'tis the Iriſh officer that parted us, and brings me young Dudley's challenge; I ſhould have made a long ſtory of it, and he'll tell you in three words.

O'FLAHERTY *enters.*

O'Fla. Save you, my dear; and you Sir! I have a little bit of a word in private for you.

Bel. Pray deliver your commands; this gentleman is my intimate friend.

O'Fla. Why then, Enſign Dudley will be glad to meaſure ſwords with you, yonder, at the London Tavern, in Biſhopſgate-Street, at nine o'clock—you know the place.

Bel. I do; and ſhall obſerve the appointment.

O'Fla. Will you be of the party, Sir? we ſhall want a fourth hand.

Stock. Savage as the cuſtom is, I cloſe with your propoſal; and tho' I am not fully inform'd of the occaſion of your quarrel, I ſhall rely on Mr. Belcour's honour for the juſtice of it; and willingly ſtake my life in his defence.

O'Fla. Sir, you're a gentleman of honour, and I ſhall be glad of being better known to you——But hark'e, Belcour, I had like to have forgot part of my errand: there is is the money you gave old Dudley; you may tell it over faith; 'tis a receipt in full; now the lad can put you to death with a safe conscience, and when he has done that job for you, let it be a warning how you attempt the sister of a man of honour.

Bel. The sister?

O'Fla. Ay, the sister; 'tis English, is it not? Or Irish; 'tis all one; you understand me, his sister, or Louisa Dudley, that's her name I think, call her which you will: by St. Patrick, 'tis a foolish piece of business, Belcour, to go about to take away a poor girl's virtue from her, when there are so many to be met with in this town, who have dispos'd of their's to your hands. [*Exit.*

Stock. Why I am thunderstruck! what is it you have done, and what is the shocking business in which I have engaged? If I understand him right, 'tis the sister of young Dudley you've been attempting: you talk'd to me of a profest wanton; the girl he speaks of has beauty enough indeed to inflame your desires, but she has honour, innocence and simplicity to awe the most licentious passion; if you have done that, Mr. Belcour, I renounce you, I abandon you, I forswear all fellowship or friendship with you for ever.

Bel. Have patience for a moment; we do indeed speak of the same person, but she is not innocent, she is not young Dudley's sister.

Stock. Astonishing! who told you this?

Bel. The woman where she lodges; the person who put me on the pursuit, and contriv'd our meetings.

Stock. What woman? What person?

Bel. Fulmer her name is: I warrant you I did not proceed without good grounds.

Stock. Fulmer, Fulmer! Who waits? (*a Servant enters*) send Mr. Stukely hither directly; I begin to see my way into this dark transaction: Mr. Belcour, Mr. Belcour, you are no match for the cunning and contrivances of this intriguing town. (Stukely *enters*) Pr'ythee, Stukely, what is the name of the woman and her husband, who were stopt upon suspicion of selling stolen diamonds at our next-door neighbour's, the jeweller?

Stukely. Fulmer.

Stock. So!

Bel. Can you procure me a sight of those diamonds?

Stukely.

Stukely. They are now in my hand; I was desir'd to show them to Mr. Stockwell.

Stock. Give 'em to me: what do I see? As I live, the very diamonds Miss Rusport sent hither, and which I intrusted to you to return.

Bel. Yes, but I betray'd that trust, and give 'em Mrs. Fulmer to present to Miss Dudley.

Stock. With a view no doubt to bribe her to compliance?

Bel. I own it.

Stock. For shame, for shame; and 'twas this woman's intelligence you relied upon for Miss Dudley's character?

Bel. I thought she knew her; by Heaven, I wou'd have died sooner than have insulted a woman of virtue, or a man of honour.

Stock. I think you wou'd, but mark the danger of licentious courses; you are betray'd, robb'd, abus'd, and, but for this providential discovery, in a fair way of being sent out of the world with all your follies on your head—Dear Stukely, go to my neighbour, tell him I have an owner for the jewels, and beg him to carry the people under custody to the London Tavern, and wait for me there.

[*Exit* Stukely.

I fear the law does not provide a punishment to reach the villainy of these people; but how in the name of wonder cou'd you take any thing on the word of such an informer?

Bel. Because I had not liv'd long enough in your country to know how few informers words are to be taken; persuaded however as I was of Miss Dudley's guilt, I must own to you I was stagger'd with the appearance of such innocence, especially when I saw her admitted into Miss Rusport's company.

Stock. Good Heaven! did you meet her at Miss Rusport's, and could you doubt her being a woman of reputation?

Bel. By you perhaps such a mistake cou'd not have been made; but in a perfect stranger, I hope it is venial; I did not know what artifices young Dudley might have us'd to conceal her character; I did not know what disgrace attended the detection of it.

Stock. I see it was a trap laid for you, which you have narrowly escap'd; you address'd a woman of honour with all

all the loose incense of a profane admirer, and you have drawn upon you the resentment of a man of honour who thinks himself bound to protect her: Well, Sir, you must atone for this mistake.

Bel. To the lady the most penitent submission I can make is justly due, but in the execution of an act of justice it never shall be said my soul was swayed by the least particle of fear: I have received a challenge from her brother; now, tho' I wou'd give my fortune, almost my life itself, to purchase her happiness, yet I cannot abate her one scruple of my honour; I have been branded with the name of villain.

Stock. Ay, Sir, you mistook her character, and he mistook yours; error begets error.

Bel. Villain, Mr. Stockwell, is a harsh word.

Stock. It is a harsh word, and should be unsaid.

Bel. Come, come, it shall be unsaid.

Stock. Or else what follows? Why the sword is drawn, and to heal the wrongs you have done to the reputation of the sister, you make an honourable amends by murdering the brother.

Bel. Murdering!

Stock. 'Tis thus religion writes and speaks the word; in the vocabulary of modern honour there is no such term —But come, I don't despair of satisfying the one without alarming the other; that done, I have a discovery to unfold that you will then I hope be fitted to receive.

END OF THE FOURTH ACT.

ACT

ACT V. SCENE I.

The London Tavern.

O'FLAHERTY, STOCKWELL, CHARLES, *and* BELCOUR.

O'FLAHERTY.

GENTLEMEN, well met! you underſtand each other's minds, and as I ſee you have brought nothing but your ſwords, you may ſet to without any further ceremony.

Stock. You will not find us backward in any worthy cauſe; but before we proceed any further, I would aſk this young gentleman, whether he has any explanation to require of Mr. Belcour.

Charles. Of Mr. Belcour none; his actions ſpeak for themſelves: but to you, ſir, I would fain propoſe one queſtion.

Stock. Name it.

Charles. How is it, Mr. Stockwell, that I meet a man of your character on this ground?

Stock. I will anſwer you directly, and my anſwer ſhall not diſpleaſe you. I come hither in defence of the reputation of Miſs Dudley, to redreſs the injuries of an innocent young lady.

O'Fla. By my ſoul the man knows he's to fight, only he miſtakes which ſide he's to be of.

Stock. You are about to draw your ſword to refute a charge againſt your ſiſter's honour; you would do well, if there were no better means within reach; but the proofs of her innocence are lodg'd in our boſoms, and if we fall, you deſtroy the evidence that moſt effectually can clear her fame.

Charles. How's that, Sir?

Stock. This gentleman could beſt explain it to you, but you have given him an undeſerv'd name that ſeals his lips againſt you: I am not under the ſame inhibition, and if your anger can keep cool for a few minutes, I deſire I may call in two witneſſes, who will ſolve all difficulties at once. Here, waiter! bring thoſe people in that are without.

O'Fla. Out upon it, what need is there for ſo much

talking about the matter; can't you ſettle your differences firſt, and diſpute about 'em afterwards?

(FULMER *and Mrs.* FULMER *brought in.*)

Charles. Fulmer and his wife in cuſtody?

Stock. Yes, Sir, theſe are your honeſt landlord and landlady, now in cuſtody for defrauding this gentleman of certain diamonds intended to have been preſented to your ſiſter. Be ſo good, Mrs. Fulmer, to inform the company why you ſo groſſly ſcandalized the reputation of an innocent lady, by perſuading Mr. Belcour that Miſs Dudley was not the ſiſter, but the miſtreſs of this gentleman.

Mrs. Ful. Sir, I don't know what right you have to queſtion me, and I ſhall not anſwer till I ſee occaſion.

Stock. Had you been as ſilent heretofore, Madam, it would have ſaved you ſome trouble; but we don't want your confeſſion. This letter, which you wrote to Mr. Belcour, will explain you deſign; and theſe diamonds, which of right belong to Miſs Ruſport, will confirm your guilt: the law, Mrs. Fulmer, will make you ſpeak, tho' I can't. Conſtable, take charge of your priſoners.

Ful. Hold a moment: Mr. Stockwell, you are a gentleman that knows the world, and a member of parliament; we ſhall not attempt to impoſe upon you; we know we are open to the law, and we know the utmoſt it can do againſt us. Mr. Belcour has been ill uſed to be ſure, and ſo has Miſs Dudley; and, for my own part, I always condemn'd the plot as a very fooliſh plot, but it was a child of Mrs. Fulmer's brain, and ſhe would not be put out of conceit with it.

Mrs. Ful. You are a fooliſh man, Mr. Fulmer, ſo pry'thee hold your tongue.

Ful. Therefore, as I was ſaying, if you ſend her to Bridewell, it won't be amiſs; and if you give her a little wholeſome diſcipline, ſhe may be the better for that too: but for me, Mr. Stockwell, who am a man of letters, I muſt beſeech you, Sir, not to bring any diſgrace upon my profeſſion.

Stock. 'Tis you, Mr. Fulmer, not I, that diſgrace your profeſſion, therefore begone, nor expect that I will betray the intereſts of mankind ſo far as to ſhew favour to ſuch incendiaries. Take 'em away; I bluſh to think ſuch

wretches

wretches ſhould have the power to ſet two honeſt men at variance. [*Exeunt* Fulmer, *&c.*

Charles. Mr. Belcour, we have miſtaken each other; let us exchange forgiveneſs. I am convinced you intended no affront to my ſiſter, and aſk your pardon for the expreſſion I was betrayed into.

Bel. 'Tis enough, Sir; the error began on my ſide, and was Miſs Dudley here, I would be firſt to atone.

Stock. Let us all adjourn to my houſe, and conclude the evening like friends: you will find a little entertainment ready for you; and, if I am not miſtaken, Miſs Dudley and her father will make part of our company. Come, Major, do you conſent?

O'Fla. Moſt readily, Mr. Stockwell; a quarrel well made up, is better than a victory hardly earned. Give me your hand, Belcour; o' my conſcience you are too honeſt for the country you live in. And now, my dear lad, ſince peace is concluded on all ſides, I have a diſcovery to make to you, which you muſt find out for yourſelf, for deuce take me if I rightly comprehend it, only that your aunt Ruſport is in a conſpiracy againſt you, and a vile rogue of a lawyer, whoſe name I forget, at the bottom of it.

Charles. What conſpiracy? Dear Major, recollect yourſelf.

O'Fla. By my ſoul, I've no faculty at recollecting myſelf; but I've a paper ſomewhere about me, that will tell you more of the matter than I can. When I get to the merchant's, I will endeavour to find it.

Charles. Well, it muſt be in your own way; but I confeſs you have thoroughly rous'd my curioſity.

[*Exeunt.*

SCENE II.

STOCKWELL'S *Houſe.*

CAPT. DUDLEY, LOUISA, *and* STUKELY.

Dud. And are thoſe wretches, Fulmer and his wife, in ſafe cuſtody?

Stuke. They are in good hands, I accompanied them to the Tavern, where your ſon was to be, and then went in ſearch of you. You may be ſure Mr. Stockwell will enforce the law againſt them as far as it will go.

Dud. What miſchief might their curſed machinations have produced, but for this timely diſcovery!

Lou. Still I am terrified; I tremble with apprehenſion leſt Mr. Belcour's impetuoſity and Charles's ſpirit ſhou'd not wait for an explanation, but drive them both to extremes; before the miſtake can be unravell'd.

Stuke. Mr. Stockwell is with them, Madam, and you have nothing to fear; you cannot ſuppoſe he would aſk you hither for any other purpoſe, but to celebrate their reconciliation and to receive Mr. Belcour's atonement.

Dud. No, no, Louiſa, Mr. Stockwell's honour and diſcretion guard you againſt all danger or offence; he well knows we will endure no imputation on the honour of our family, and he certainly has invited us to receive ſatisfaction on that ſcore in an amicable way.

Lou. Wou'd to Heaven they were return'd!

Stuke. You may expect them every minute; and ſee Madam, agreeably to you wiſh, they are here. [*Exit.*

SCENE III.

CHARLES *enters, and afterwards* STOCKWELL *and* O'FLAHERTY.

Lou. O Charles, O brother, how cou'd you ſerve me ſo, how cou'd you tell me you was going to Lady Ruſport's and then ſet out with a deſign of fighting Mr. Belcour? But where is he: where is your antagoniſt?

Stock. Captain, I am proud to ſee you, and you Miſs Dudley, do me particular honour: We have been adjuſting, Sir, a very extraordinary and dangerous miſtake, which I take for granted my friend Stukely has explain'd to you.

Dud. He has; I have too good an opinion of Mr. Belcour to believe he cou'd be guilty of a deſign'd affront to an innocent girl, and I am much too well acquainted with your character to ſuppoſe you cou'd abet him in ſuch deſign; I have no doubt therefore all things will be ſet to rights in very few words when we have the pleaſure of ſeeing Mr. Belcour.

Stock.

Stock. He has only ſtept into the compting-houſe and will wait upon you directly: You will not be over ſtrict, Madam, in weighing Mr. Belcour's conduct to the minuteſt ſcruple; his manners, paſſions and opinions are not as yet aſſimilated to this climate; he comes amongſt you a new character, an inhabitant of a new world, and both hoſpitality as well as pity recommend him to our indulgence.

SCENE IV.

BELCOUR *enters, bows to* MISS DUDLEY.

Bel. I am happy and aſham'd to ſee you; no man in his ſenſes wou'd offend you; I forfeited mine and err'd againſt the light of the ſun, when I overlook'd your virtues; but your beauty was predominant, and hid them from my ſight; I now perceive I was the dupe of a moſt improbable report, and humbly entreat your pardon.

Lou. Think no more of it; 'twas a miſtake.

Bel. My life has been compos'd of little elſe; 'twas founded in myſtery, and has continued in error: I was once given to hope, Mr. Stockwell, that you was to have deliver'd me from theſe difficulties, but either I do not deſerve your confidence, or I was deceived in my expectations.

Stock. When this lady has confirm'd your pardon, I ſhall hold you deſerving of my confidence.

Lou. That was granted the moment it was aſk'd.

Bel. To prove my title to his confidence, honour me ſo far with your's as to allow me a few minutes converſation in private with you. [*She turns to her father.*

Dud. By all means, Louiſa; come, Mr. Stockwell, let us go into another room.

Charles. And now, Major O'Flaherty, I claim your promiſe of a ſight of the paper, that is to unravel this conſpiracy of my aunt Ruſport's: I think I have waited with great patience.

O'Fla. I have been endeavouring to call to mind what it was I overheard; I've got the paper, and will give you the beſt account I can of the whole tranſaction.

[*Exeunt.*

SCENE V.

BELCOUR *and* LOUISA.

Bel. Miſs Dudley, I have ſolicited this audience to repeat to you my penitence and confuſion: How ſhall I atone? What reparation can I make to you and virtue?

Lou. To me there's nothing due, nor any thing demanded of you but your more favourable opinion for the future, if you ſhould chance to think of me: Upon the part of virtue I'm not empower'd to ſpeak, but if hereafter, as you range thro' life, you ſhou'd ſurprize her in the perſon of ſome wretched female, poor as myſelf, and not ſo well protected, enforce not your advantage, compleat not your licentious triumph, but raiſe her, reſcue her from ſhame and ſorrow, and reconcile her to herſelf again.

Bel. I will, I will; by bearing your idea ever preſent in my thoughts, virtue ſhall keep an advocate within me: but tell me, lovelieſt, when you pardon the offence, can you, all perfect as you are, approve of the offender? As I now ceaſe to view you in that falſe light I lately did, can you, and in the fulneſs of your bounty will you, ceaſe alſo to reflect upon the libertine addreſſes I have paid you, and look upon me as your reform'd, your rational admirer?

Lou. Are ſudden reformations apt to laſt? and how can I be ſure the firſt fair face you meet will not enſnare affections ſo unſteady, and that I ſhall not loſe you lightly as I gain'd you?

Bel. Becauſe tho' you conquer'd me by ſurprize, I have no inclination to rebel; becauſe ſince the firſt moment that I ſaw you, every inſtant has improv'd you in my eyes, becauſe by principle as well as paſſion I am unalterably your's; in ſhort there are ten thouſand cauſes for my love to you, would to Heaven I could plant one in your ſoft boſom that might move you to return it!

Lou Nay, Mr. Belcour——

Bel. I know I am not worthy your regard; I know I'm tainted with a thouſand faults, ſick of a thouſand follies, but there's a healing virtue in your eyes that makes recovery certain; I cannot be a villain in your arms.

Lou. That you can never be; whomever you ſhall honour with your choice, my life upon't that woman will

will be happy; it is not from suspicion that I hesitate, it is from honour; 'tis the severity of my condition, it is the world that never will interpret fairly in our case.

Bel. Oh, what am I, and who in this wide world concerns himself for such a nameless, such a friendless thing as I am? I see, Miss Dudley, I've not yet obtain'd your pardon.

Lou. Nay, that you are in full possession of.

Bel. Oh, seal it with your hand then, loveliest of women, confirm it with your heart; make me honourably happy, and crown your penitent not with your pardon only, but your love.

Lou. My love!——

Bel. By Heav'n my soul is conquer'd with your virtues more than my eyes are ravish'd with your beauty: Oh, may this soft, this sensitive alarm be happy, be auspicious! Doubt not, deliberate not, delay not: If happiness be the end of life, why do we slip a moment?

SCENE VI.

O'FLAHERTY *enters, and afterwards* DUDLEY *and* CHARLES *with* STOCKWELL.

O'Fla. Joy, joy, joy! sing, dance, leap, laugh for joy! Ha' done making love, and fall down on your knees to every saint in the calendar, for they're all on your side, and honest St. Patrick at the head of them.

Charles. O Louisa, such an event! by the luckiest chance in life we have discover'd a will of my grandfather's made in his last illness, by which he cuts off my aunt Rusport with a small annuity, and leaves me heir to his whole estate, with a fortune of fifteen thousand pounds to yourself.

Lou. What is it you tell me? O Sir, instruct me to support this unexpected turn of fortune. [*To her father.*

Dud. Name not fortune; 'tis the work of Providence, 'tis the justice of Heaven that wou'd not suffer innocence to be oppress'd, nor your base aunt to prosper in her cruelty and cunning.

[*A servant whispers* BELCOUR, *and he goes out.*

O'Fla.

O'Fla. You ſhall pardon me, Captain Dudley, but you muſt not overlook St. Patrick neither, for by my ſoul if he had not put it into my head to ſlip behind the ſcreen when your righteous aunt and the lawyer were plotting together, I don't ſee how you wou'd ever have come at the paper there, that Maſter Stockwell is reading.

Dud. True my good friend, you are the father of this diſcovery, but how did you contrive to get this will from the lawyer?

O'Fla. By force, my dear, the only way of getting any thing from a lawyer's clutches.

Stock. Well, Major, when he brings his action of aſſault and battery againſt you, the leaſt Dudley can do is to defend you with the weapons you have put into his hands.

Charles. That I am bound to do, and after the happineſs I ſhall have in ſheltering a father's age from the viciſſitudes of life, my next delight will be in offering you an aſylum in the boſom of your country.

O'Fla. And upon my ſoul, my dear, 'tis high time I was there, for 'tis now thirty long years ſince I ſat foot in my native country, and by the power of St. Patrick I ſwear I think it's worth all the reſt of the world put together.

Dud. Ay, Major, much about that time have I been beating the round of ſervice, and 'twere well for us both to give over; we have ſtood many a tough gale and abundance of hard blows, but Charles ſhall lay us up in a little private, but ſafe, harbour, where we'll reſt from our labours, and peacefully wind up the remainder of our days

O'Fla. Agreed, and you may take it as a proof of my eſteem, young man, that Major O'Flaherty accepts a favour at your hands, for by Heaven I'd ſooner ſtarve, than ſay I thank you to the man I deſpiſe: But I believe you are an honeſt lad, and I'm glad you've trounc'd the old cat, for on my conſcience I believe I muſt otherwiſe have married her myſelf to have let you in for a ſhare of her fortune.

Stock. Hey-day, what's become of Belcour?

Lou. One of your ſervants call'd him out juſt now, and ſeemingly on ſome earneſt occaſion.

Stock.

Stock. I hope, Miſs Dudley, he has aton'd to you as a gentleman ought.

Lou. Mr. Belcour, Sir, will always do what a gentleman ought, and in my caſe I fear only you will think he has done too much.

Stock. What has he done; and what can be too much? Pray Heaven, it may be as I wiſh! [*aſide.*

Dud. Let us hear it, child.

Lou. With confuſion for my own unworthineſs, I confeſs to you he has offer'd me——

Stock. Himſelf.

Lou. 'Tis true.

Stock. Then I am happy; all my doubts; my cares are over, and I may own him for my ſon.——Why theſe are joyful tidings: come, my good friend, aſſiſt me in diſpoſing your lovely daughter to accept this returning prodigal; he is no unprincipled, no harden'd libertine; his love for you and virtue is the ſame.

Dud. 'Twere vile ingratitude in me to doubt his merit —What ſays my child?

O'Fla. Begging you pardon now, 'tis a frivolous ſort of a queſtion, that of your's; for you may ſee plainly enough by the young lady's looks, that ſhe ſays a great deal, though ſhe ſpeaks never a word.

Charles. Well, ſiſter, I believe the Major has fairly interpreted the ſtate of your heart.

Lou. I own it; and what muſt that heart be, which love, honour, and beneficence like Mr. Belcour's can make no impreſſion on?

Stock. I thank you: What happineſs has this hour brought to paſs.

O'Fla. Why don't we all ſit down to ſupper then and make a night on't.

Stock. Hold, here comes Belcour.

SCENE VII.

BELCOUR *introducing* MISS RUSPORT.

Bel. Mr. Dudley, here is a fair refugee, who properly comes under your protection; ſhe is equipt for Scotland, but your good fortune, which I have related to her, ſeems inclin'd to ſave you both the journey——Nay, Madam, never go back; you are amongſt friends.

Charles. Charlotte!

Char. The ſame; that fond officious girl, that haunts you every where; that perſecuting ſpirit——

Charles. Say rather, that protecting angel; ſuch you have been to me.

Char. O Charles, you have an honeſt, but proud heart.

Charles. Nay, chide me not, dear Charlotte.

Bel. Seal up her lips then; ſhe is an adorable girl; her arms are open to you; and love and happineſs are ready to receive you.

Charles. Thus then I claim my dear, my deſtin'd wife. [*embracing her.*

SCENE VIII.

LADY RUSPORT *enters.*

L. Ruſ. Heyday! mighty fine! wife truly! mighty well! kiſſing, embracing—did ever any thing equal this? Why you ſhameleſs huſſey!—But I won't condeſcend to waſte a word upon you ——You, Sir, you, Mr. Stockwell, you fine, ſanctified, fair-dealing man of conſcience, is this the principle you trade upon? Is this your neighbourly ſyſtem, to keep a houſe of reception for run-away daughters, and young beggarly fortune-hunters?

O'Fla. Be adviſ'd now, and don't put yourſelf in ſuch a paſſion; we were all very happy till you came.

L. Ruſ. Stand away, Sir; hav'nt I a reaſon to be in a paſſion?

O'Fla. Indeed, honey, and you have, if you knew all.

L. Ruſ. Come, Madam, I have found out your haunts; diſpoſe yourſelf to return home with me: young man, let me never ſee you within my doors again: Mr. Stockwell, I ſhall report your behaviour, depend on it.

Stock. Hold, Madam, I cannot conſent to loſe Miſs Ruſport's company this evening, and I am perſuaded you won't inſiſt upon it; 'tis an unmotherly action to interrupt your daughter's happineſs in this manner, believe me it is.

L. Ruſ. Her happineſs truly: upon my word! and I ſuppoſe it's an unmotherly action to interrupt her ruin; for what but ruin muſt it be to marry a beggar? I think my ſiſter had a proof of that, Sir, when ſhe made choice of you. [*To* CAPT. DUDLEY.

Dud.

Dud. Don't be too lavifh of your fpirits, Lady Rufport.

O'Fla. By my foul you'll have occafion for a fip of the cordial elixir by and by.

Stock. It don't appear to me, Madam, that Mr. Dudley can be called a beggar.

L. Ruf. But it appears to me, Mr. Stockwell; I am apt to think a pair of colours cannot furnifh fettlement quite fufficient for the heirefs of Sir Stephen Rufport.

Char. But a good eftate in aid of a commiffion may do fomething.

L. Ruf. A good eftate, truly! where fhou'd he get a good eftate pray?

Stock. Why fuppofe now a worthy old gentleman on his death-bed fhould have taken it in mind to leave him one——

L. Ruf. Hah! what's that you fay?

O'Fla. O ho! you begin to fmell a plot, do you?

Stock. Suppofe there fhould be a paper in the world that runs thus—"I do hereby give and bequeath all my eftates, "real and perfonal, to Charles Dudley, fon of my late "daughter Louifa, &c. &c. &c."

L. Ruf. Why I am thunder ftruck! by what contrivance, what villainy did you get poffeffion of that paper?

Stock. There was no villainy, Madam, in getting poffeffion of it; the crime was in concealing it, none in bringing it to light.

L. Ruf. Oh, that curfed lawyer, Varland!

O'Fla. You may fay that, faith, he is a curfed lawyer; and a curfed piece of work I had to get the paper from him; your ladyfhip now was to have paid him five thoufand pounds for it, I forc'd him to give it me of his own accord for nothing at all, at all.

L. Ruf. Is it you that have done this? Am I foil'd by your blundering contrivances, after all?

O'Fla. 'Twas a blunder, faith, but as natural a one as if I'd made it o' purpofe.

Charles. Come, let us not opprefs the fallen; do right even now, and you fhall have no caufe to complain.

L. Ruf. Am I become an object of your pity then? Infufferable! confufion light amongft you! marry and be wretched: let me never fee you more. [*Exit.*

L 2 *Char.*

Char. She is outrageous; I suffer for her, and blush to see her thus exposed.

Charles. Come, Charlotte, don't let this angry woman disturb our happiness: we will save her in spite of herself; your father's memory shall not be stained by the discredit of his second choice.

Char. I trust implicitly to your discretion, and am in all things yours.

Bel. Now, lovely but obdurate, does not this example soften?

Lou. What can you ask for more? Accept my hand, accept my willing heart.

Bel. O bliss unutterable! brother, father, friend, and you the author of this general joy—

O'Fla. Blessing of St. Patrick upon us all! 'tis a night of wonderful and surprizing ups and downs: I wish we were all fairly set down to supper, and there was an end on't.

Stock. Hold for a moment! I have yet one word to interpose—Intitled by my friendship to a voice in your disposal, I have approv'd your match; there yet remains a father's consent to be obtain'd.

Bel. Have I a father?

Stock. You have a father: did not I tell you I had a discovery to make? Compose yourself: you have a father, who observes, who knows, who loves you.

Bel. Keep me no longer in suspense; my heart is soften'd for the affecting discovery, and nature fits me to receive his blessing.

Stock. I am your father.

Bel. My father? Do I live?

Stock. I am your father.

Bel. It is too much; my happiness o'erpowers me; to gain a friend and find a father is too much; I blush to think how little I deserve you. [*They embrace.*

Dud. See, children, how many new relations spring from this night's unforeseen events, to endear us to each other.

O'Fla. O my conscience, I think we shall be all related by and bye.

Stock. How happily has this evening concluded, and yet how threatening was its approach! let us repair to the supper room, where I will unfold to you every circumstance of

my

my myſterious ſtory. Yes, Belcour, I have watch'd you with a patient, but enquiring eye, and I have diſcover'd through the veil of ſome irregularities, a heart beaming with benevolence, and animated nature, fallible indeed, but not incorrigible; and your election of this excellent young lady makes me glory in acknowledging you to be my ſon.

Bel. I thank you, and in my turn glory in the father I have gained: ſenſibly impreſt with gratitude for ſuch extraordinary diſpenſations, I beſeech you, amiable Louiſa, for the time to come, whenever you perceive me deviating into error or offence, bring only to my mind the Providence of this night, and I will turn to reaſon and obey.

END OF THE PLAY.

E P I L O G U E.

Written by D. G. Esq.

SPOKEN BY MRS. ABINGTON.

N. B. The Lines in Italics are to be spoken in a catechise Tone.

CONFESS, good folks, has not Miss Rusport shewn,
Strange whims for SEVENTEEN HUNDRED SEVENTY-ONE?
What, pawn her jewels!——there's a precious plan!
To extricate from want a brave *old* man;
And fall in love with poverty and honour;
A girl of fortune, fashion!——Fie upon her.
But do not think we females of the stage,
So dead to the refinements of the age,
That we agree with our old fashioned poet:
I am point blank against him, and I'll shew it:
And that my tongue may more politely run,
Make me a lady———Lady Blabington.
Now, with a rank and title to be free,
I'll make a catechism—and you shall see,
What is the *veritable Beaume de Vie:*
As I change place, I stand for that, or this,
My Lady questions first——then answers Miss.

(She speaks as my Lady.)

" Come, tell me Child, what were our modes and dress,
" In those strange times of that old fright Queen Bess?"
And now for Miss———

(She changes place, and speaks for Miss.)

When Bess was England's queen,
Ladies were dismal beings, seldom seen;
These rose betimes, and breakfasted as soon
On beef and beer, then studied Greek till noon;
Unpainted cheeks with blush of health did glow,
Beruff'd and fardingal'd from top to toe,
Nor necks, nor ancles would they ever shew.

Learnt Greek!—*(laughs.)*—Our outside head takes half a day;
Have we much time to dress the *inside*, pray?
No heads dress'd *à la Greque*; the ancients quote,
There may be learning in a *papillote*:

Cards

Cards are *our* classicks; and I, Lady B,
In learning will not yield to any she,
Of the late founded *female* university.
But now for Lady Blab——

(Speaks as my Lady.)

"Tell me, Miss Nancy,
"What sports and what employments did they fancy!"

(Speaks as Miss.)

The vulgar creatures seldom left their houses,
But taught their children, work'd, and lov'd their spouses;
The use of cards at Christmas only knew,
They play'd for little, and their games were few,
One-and-thirty, Put, All-fours, and Lantera-Loo:
They bore a race of mortals stout and boney,
And never heard the name of Macaroni.——

(Speaks as my Lady.)

"Oh brava, brava! that's my pretty dear——
"Now let a modern, modish fair appear;
"No more of these old dowdy maids and wives,
"Tell how superior beings pass their lives."——

(Speaks as Miss.)

Till noon they sleep, from noon till night they dress,
From night till morn they game it more or less,
Next night the same sweet course of joy run o'er,
Then the night after as the night before,
And the night after that, encore, encore!——

(She comes forward.)

Thus with our cards we *shuffle* off all sorrow,
To-morrow, and to-morrow, and to-morrow!
We *deal apace*, from youth unto our prime,
To the last moment of our *tabby*-time;
And all our yesterdays, from rout and drum,
Have lighted fools with empty pockets home.
Thus do our lives with rapture roll away,
Not with the nonsense of our author's play;
This is true life—true spirit—give it praise;
Don't snarl and sigh for good Queen Bess's days:
For all you look so sour, and bend the brow,
You all rejoice with me, you're living now.